I0104557

WRITING FROM WITHIN:

TAPPING THE CREATIVE UNCONSCIOUS

How to Use Your Subconscious Mind

To Supercharge Your Creative Writing

By Mark W. Curran

With a Foreword

by Isaac Asimov

NMD Books
Simi Valley, CA

Copyright 2011 – Mark W. Curran
All rights reserved. No part of this book may be reproduced in any
format or by any means without written permission from the
publisher.

For Information, contact NMD Books,
2828 Cochran Street, Suite 285 Simi Valley, CA 93065.

Visit our Web site at
http://www.NMDbooks.com

Library of Congress Control Number: 2011923194

Writing From Within: Tapping The Creative Unconscious
Subtitle: How to Use Your Subconscious Mind
To Supercharge Your Creative Writing

ISBN: 978-1-936828-16-6 (Softcover)

First Edition February 2011

"Imagination is the outreaching of mind . . . . the bombardment of the conscious mind with ideas, impulses, images and every sort of psychic phenomena welling up from the preconscious. It is the capacity to dream dreams and see visions."

- *Rollo May*

TABLE OF CONTENTS

FOREWORD

Writers since the beginning of time have used their subconscious minds to conjure images up from the depths of the psyche. It is essential in the creative process to pull from within, and then apply that in an empathic way. In order for readers to identify and see within themselves the plight of the hero, the writer must touch the truth and heart of an emotion.

The writer must enable us to see and feel vividly what his characters see and feel; that is, enable us to experience as directly and intensely as possible, though vicariously, what his characters experience. ... The writer must of necessity write in a style that falls somewhere on the continuum running from objective to subjective; in other words, from the discursive, essayist's style, in which everything is spelled out as scientifically as possible, to the poetic style, in which nothing (or practically nothing) is explained, everything is evoked, or, to use Henry James' term, "rendered." ...

Wherever the writer's style falls on the continuum running from objective to subjective, what counts is conventional fiction must be the vividness and continuity of the fictional dream the words set off in the reader's mind. The writer's characters must stand before us with a wonderful clarity, such continuous clarity that nothing they do strikes us as improbable behavior for just that character, even when the character's action is, as sometimes happens, something that came as a surprise to the writer himself.

We must understand, and the writer before us must understand, more than we know about the character; otherwise neither the writer nor the reader after him could feel confident of the character's behavior when the character acts freely.

If it is true that no two writers get aesthetic interest from exactly the same materials, yet true that all writers, given adequate technique, can stir our interest in their special subject matter--since all human beings have the same root experience (we're born, we suffer, we die, to put it grimly), so that all we need for our sympathy to be roused is that the writer communicate with power and conviction the similarities in his characters' experience and our own--then it must follow that the first business of the writer must be to make us see and feel vividly what his characters see and feel.

However odd, however wildly unfamiliar the fictional world--odd as hog-farming to a fourth generation Parisian designer, or Wall Street to an unemployed tuba player--we must be drawn into the characters' world as if we were born to it.

The subconscious contains all the imagery of the cosmos. The writer, and, in a larger context, the creative source within all of us, must learn ways to access this vast river of universal knowledge and emotion to express and create order from the chaos of a seemingly meaningless universe.

- Isaac Asimov

Introduction

While doing research on the subject of using the power of the subconscious mind in creative writing, I'd uncovered a rich vein of knowledge from a variety of disciplines.

From research scientists, psychologists, sociologists, anthropologists and philosophers to scholars, existentialists, mystics and even magicians.

Many very famous writers, from Faulkner to Hemingway, to more contemporary scribes such as Stephen King, Harlan Ellison and my dear (late) friend Isaac Asimov, have talked extensively about the use of the subconscious in the writer's toolkit.

One thing became certain: that all of us, no matter from what walk of life, holds the power of the creative spirit and the power of the subconscious mind within ourselves.

It's unclear just how the process works, and from what deep recesses of the psyche our ideas flow.

What is clear is that there is a creative force in all of us. To be creative is as natural to our state of being as growth is to a flower, and if this creative process is not allowed to flourish, we become moody, unfulfilled and frustrated.

What this book has set out to accomplish is to understand and use the dynamic power of creativity in your writing, through the use of your inner voice and your subconscious mind.

It touches on some areas such as philosophy, psychology and physiology, but it is not meant as a comprehensive scientific treatise. (I also carefully avoid the subject of story structure, character and plotting, all subjects best addressed in other books.)

I like to think of it as a nuts and bolts manual on getting into the creative core of your being and getting that out onto paper.

We'll explore methods for stimulating and utilizing that creative muse, as well as use real world examples and tools, tricks and exercises for mining the gold that lies deep beneath the surface of your psyche.

While it sounds mythical, mystical and complex (and in a sense it is), understanding the process is not as important as applying it.

This works on the same principle that understanding the mechanics of the internal combustion engine is not needed to drive a car to your destination.

And while we're using that analogy, remember, it's not the destination but the journey that's most important.

Writing is the key to our immortality. Our communion with the creative unconscious is our connection to Spirit.

This book is dedicated to learning and understanding the process to tap into that great wellspring of imagination – the creative unconscious.

Mark W. Curran
Los Angeles - 2011

1

The Psychology and Philosophy of Creation

What is creativity? How does it happen? How is it that creativity is manifest in discovery as well as invention, in science as well as art? What role does creativity play in the construction of the self?

Many researchers have studied the field of creativity over the years, and its relation to the subconscious mind.

All of us, no matter what our origins, feel the need to create. Creativity is not limited to the arts by any means. It's used in all aspects of life.
In this book, we'll focus primarily on creativity and its use in your creative writing.

Not to belabor the mechanics behind how it works, but just knowing that it works, and the more we stay out of its way, the better off we'll be.

Silencing the inner critic and just letting the ideas flow from the subconscious mind into the conscious mind and then out on to the paper is our goal.

The psychology behind this act is pretty simple and straightforward: we wish to empower ourselves and to give purpose and meaning to our lives by taking our observations, ideas and points of view and place them in an order of contextual meaning.

In so doing we have created something where there was once nothing, and hence we have allowed to bring into being a new form. This is an elemental force of nature.

All of life does it without thought or conscious-ness, but our plight is different. We are seeking to *consciously* and deliberately take from the universe symbols, ideas, building blocks of character, story, song or color and weave them into a tapestry of our own design.

To make them our own, to make them unique, and then share them with the world. (or, if the fates are unkind, or our inner critic does not allow their release, keep them in a drawer locked away forever.)

Just exactly what drives us to create is a subject for the psychologists, but probably for our sake, its best we not think too much about why, and just go with the flow that it's just an elemental force of our own inner self seeking expression.

The philosophy behind it solicits a lot of different opinions, but let's suffice to say for our own purposes that, philosophically-speaking we do it to become immortal, to beat the undertaker at his own game.

We all wish that long after we perish in body from this planet, it is hoped we were able to leave something behind that will entertain, enrich or educate others to make their own journeys a little easier, lighter, more fun, or even profound.

Each of us wants to make a difference to those other among us or who will proceed us, and as writers, this is our vehicle. So whether you are writing poetry, short stories, novels, screenplays – you name it, it's a shot at being remembered long after we're gone. And maybe even make a million or two while we're at it.

In broad terms, everything a writer or any other creative artist needs to know about the psyche can be stated in a pair of linked propositions:

1. Your psyche – your entire inner world of thoughts, memories, emotions, drives, etc. – is comprised of two major levels, the conscious and unconscious minds, each of which plays its own discrete and proper role in the creative act.

2. Your best gambit is to regard the unconscious mind as a separate presence, a personified entity with which you work in collaboration. And that's it. That's the whole truth in a bullet-pointed nutshell. What follows is just elaboration.

The Ghost In The Attic

Through a dozen years of writing for publication and pursuing another major artistic tangent (music) on the side, I've learned that a working knowledge of the psyche – how it's composed, how it operates – is indispensable to creative success.

Obviously, I'm not alone in this. Every successful creator knows something about basic psychological reality. But not all of this knowledge is equal. Some know it only intuitively. Others know it consciously. Some of the greatest writers and artists in history have let the deep psychology of their creative activity remain perpetually vague. This is perfectly fine; there's something to be said for deliberately embracing an attitude of mystery when it comes to such subtle and profound matters. Consider, for example, Lewis Thomas's fine words in his essay about the virtues of abandoning psychotherapy in favor of voluntarily repressing our psychic contents:

"It has been one of the great errors of our time that to think that by thinking about thinking, and then talking about it, we could possibly straighten out and tidy up our minds. There is no delusion more damaging than to get the idea in your head that you understand the functioning of your own brain.

Once you acquire such a notion, you run the danger of moving in to take charge, guiding your thoughts, shepherding your mind from place to place, controlling it, making lists of regulations. The human mind is not meant to be governed, certainly not by any book of rules yet written; it is supposed to run itself, and we are obliged to follow it along, trying to keep up with it as best we can. It is all very well to be aware of your awareness, even proud of it, but never try to operate it. You are not up to the job.

. . . . We might, by this way [i.e., by deliberately hiding from ourselves a portion of our psyches], regain the kind of spontaneity and zest for ideas, things popping into the mind, uncontrollable and ungovernable thoughts, the feel that this notion is somehow connected unaccountably with that one. "

– *Lewis Thomas, "The Attic of the Brain," in Late Night Thoughts on Listening to Mahler's Ninth Symphony (1983)*

A conscious understanding of creative psychology is the most reliable way to grow your ability to negotiate between your two minds and thus achieve maximum vitality in your art. You don't have to worry that a conscious knowledge of your psychological makeup will destroy the mystery that tantalizes and drives you on.

By means of hard application one can understand the psyche and still gain the inestimable benefits of the inner vitality and spontaneity of thought that Lewis rightly cherishes. This fruitful paradox is built into the very concept of the "demon muse" under whose shadow and moniker we are gathered here.

Ray Bradbury, who in addition to being a bona fide living legend is one of the most openly and passionately muse-based writers around, spoke directly of this potent fusion of knowledge and mystery in a 2004 interview he granted to Fox News:

FoxNews.com: How did you come up with the images of Mars and Martians that are so vivid in "The Martian Chronicles" and your other works?

Bradbury: Well, you either have an imaginative mind or you don't. All of my writing is God-given. I don't write my stories — they write themselves. So out of my imagination, I create

these wonderful things, and I look at them and say, My God, did I write that?

Foxnews.com: So they all just came to you? You can't explain it?

Bradbury: Everything comes to me. Everything is my demon muse. I have a muse which whispers in my ear and says, "Do this, do that," but it's my demon who provokes me.

– "An Interview with Sci-Fi Legend Ray Bradbury," November 23, 2004

Four Steps of the Creative Process

Graham Wallas, in his work Art of Thought, published in 1926, presented one of the first models of the creative process. In the Wallas stage model, creative insights and illuminations may be explained by a process consisting of four stages:

1. Preparation
2. Incubation
3. Illumination
4. Implementation

In the preparation stage, it's kind of like a "brainstorming" exercise: if you're a writer, for example, this means looking at old pieces of work and trying to decide where to go from there. In "preparation," this might feel like work, but you're actually just trying to see what you can come up with. People usually have to do this anyway or else nothing gets done - the brainstorming might be slight, but it IS preparation for the next stage, which is incubation.

In step two, incubation, necessary connections are made in order to "lay" the idea – like when an egg is getting "incubated" and getting the heat it needs to turn into a full-blown chick. In this stage, you have the idea, but you're just giving it some steam and energy in order for it to fully materialize.

Step three is illumination, which is in short, the "lightbulb" moment. This is the time when the puzzle of an idea has come together and there's no stopping its influence from coming out in creativity. These moments sometimes happen at the most inopportune times, like when you're nowhere near a canvas, a computer, or a piece of paper. For example, this is the moment for a writer when an idea just hits them and they need to grab a piece of paper in order to remember it. Illumination means seeing the light and the creative juice is flowing its best when this "eureka!" happens.

The last step of the creative process is implementation, which means that the idea has gone down on paper – in short, this is the "final product" stage of the creativity process. For example, this is when a writer records their idea for a story and actually gets to decide if it's worth following through with.

Revelation – Insight and the Aha Moment

Although the creative act involves many stages and levels, all move toward the coveted "Aha!" moment – that flash of inspiration and insight some call revelation.
Sometimes this moment is a simple idea, a seed that seems to spring forth from nowhere. Other times, it's the solution to an ongoing creative challenge that has intrigued and teased the mind over time.

This is usually the moment where thoughts from the unconscious mind cross over into awareness, into the conscious mind. (We will address the subject of conscious and unconscious states of awareness a bit later in the book.)

This is really akin to finding the motherload, that rich vein of gold in the creative process. Many times it will impel us forward with great zeal and energy, inspired by this sudden flash of insight.

Inventors, painters, writers, scientists – virtually anyone striving within creative endeavor can become so immersed in the stages to follow they can become oblivious to time itself and become caught up in the act of bringing the creative work to fruition.

Edison was often said to shutter himself in his workshop while feverishly working on a problem or invention and shun food or human contact until he had worked through the problem or finished a particular stage in this process.

History shows us that sages and scribes from all eras of time immemorial have succumbed to this state in one form or another, and when they have, they have "lost themselves in the moment of creation."

What researchers have found is that many times, the "aha" moment comes not during the process of hard work in forging through the development stage of a problem or idea, but actually during the relaxation stage which follows.

There appears to be a gestation period in which the seed of an idea must grow and mature before it finally springs from its shell, emerging into consciousness as the aha moment.

The hard work, anxiety and frustration that goes into striving toward that revelatory moment is the true sweat of creative labor, and it's the thing that not only makes the aha moment possible, but also contains within it the madness and anxiety that drives artists and creative people into fits of frustration.

It's the journey, without question, full of detours, ruts, bad weather and trolls at the bridge. The trick is to understand that this is a necessary part of the trip, and to revel in it, to enjoy the ride, at least as much as possible, and know it's all a part of the process.

Hard, yes.

As professional athletes know, it's a long hard struggle to get to athletic mastery. But they don't turn away from the challenge.

It's as the old saying goes, "Everyone wants to get to Heaven but nobody wants to die."

This is why it's important to not wait for inspiration to strike before you begin the hard work of writing. If you sit around and wait for the spirit to move you, there's a pretty good chance it won't.

You have to suit up and show up and do the work while waiting for the creative muse to strike, which is why most professional writers and artists

I know keep a regular writing schedule, and stick to it whether they are in the mood to work or not.

> **"The job of the poet is not to wait until the cry gathers in the throat." - Archibald MacLeish**

Stephen King, the famous novelist, in his wonderful book on writing, said:

"Amateurs sit and wait for inspiration, the rest of us just get up and go to work."

— *Stephen King (On Writing)*

I don't think it's a matter of 'amateur' or 'professional,' creativity doesn't have a caste system, but if you are a person who wishes to explore and express your artistic, creative self, you will likely get the best results if you put in a regular schedule of working at your particular creative endeavor each day.

You will likely find that in many cases, your greatest insights will come after you have worked hard at working out a particular problem or story point.

This leads us back to the unconscious and conscious mind, since below the surface of our conscious minds, there is a rich and limitless world of intelligence going on that we are not aware of.

That intelligence works in the background of things and turns seeds into ideas. It is our job to help stimulate the unconscious mind, to tap into its rich resources to bring our most brilliant creations to fruition.

Anxiety and Creativity

Psychologists know from research studies that anxiety is an essential part of the creative process. Creative persons know it instinctually, and tend to avoid the creative process for just that reason.

We are pleasure seeking creatures, and will avoid pain whenever possible. But deep down inside, the artist's soul yearns for expression in the creative act. Much the same as the irritation of a grain of sand in the oyster's shell produces a beautiful pearl, so too this tension brings about the jewel of creation.

What causes the anxiety?

Some of it is just the anxiety of knowing that there will be a tension within the psyche between the desired result and the actual outcome.

Rollo May, the famed psychologist, examined this anxiety in his book "The Courage to Create."

"The fundamental contradiction arising from the hopeless discrepancy between conception and realization is at the root of all artistic creation and it helps to explain the anguish which seems to be an unavoidable component of that experience."

This might explain the misery of many artists who struggle with the anxiety of creation, yet continually do so to experience the heights of ecstasy it can produce.

Further, Rollo May writes:

"Creative people, as I see them, are distinguished by the fact that they can live with anxiety, even though a high price may be paid in terms of insecurity, sensitivity, and defenselessness for the gift of 'divine madness,' to borrow the term used by the classical Greeks.

"They do not run away from non-being, but by encountering and wrestling with it, force it to produce being. They knock on silence for an answering music; they pursue meaninglessness until they can force it to mean."

Some of the anxiety we experience when we undertake the act of creative writing arises from fear: fear of failure, fear of criticism, fear of facing one's inner demons. But the brave writer knows, as in all things in life, that inner conflict always accompanies growth.

Get behind that fear, and use it for driving your writing forward.

Creativity is Essential To Purpose

As human beings, we seek purpose and meaning in our lives. The act of creativity helps us to achieve that purpose and meaning. By creating order out of chaos, by placing the building blocks one on top of the other, we create structure and form. It is the expression of Self, and our world around us is a reflection of that.

Fly over any city at night and marvel at the expression of man's creativity. The ancient renaissance period of Italy demonstrates it even more dramatically: it was period where the expression of creativity was honored and celebrated in art, architecture, even in the building of the cities.

We are builders, striving toward the expression of our innermost selves through outward expansion. The universe, in physics and chemistry, works on the same principle.

Get behind this energy, revel in it, and know you are at one with ever expanding cosmos in expressing it.

Creativity as Religious Experience

As human beings, we seek purpose and meaning in our lives. The act of creativity helps us to achieve that purpose and meaning. By creating order out of chaos.

Larry Mullins, a writer and artist, had this to say about Creativity and the Religious Experience:

For many years I have made a living as an illustrator, graphic artist and by creative writing. I have taught many classes on creativity. I have told a few people the ultimate secret of creativity, but never published it until now.

"When people would ask me, "How do you draw a picture?" I always responded with a question. "What is your telephone number?" A bit puzzled, people always responded with their number. I then would always say the same thing: "What was it that looked for that number, and where did it find it?" Of course, they can't answer.

The truth is, no scientist, philosopher or theologian can answer that question. We have no idea how the mind works. We do not know where the drive to create comes from, nor how it successfully manifests."

We do know that there are two stages to creativity: the inspiration, the gift, or the idea, is the first stage. Everyone gets inspirations. Lots of them. It is my belief that the most lofty of these ideas come from God, or more precisely, the Universe Mother Spirit. There is no problem with finding noble inspirations, normal human minds are invaded by them constantly. It is the second stage of creativity where most of us stumble. As T. S. Elliott put it, "Between the idea and the reality ... falls the shadow."

The ultimate secret, the difference between a creative artist and the average person is very simple. The creative artist shows up. Every single day. At the easel, the writing desk, the kitchen, the nursery, or the classroom. They show up, and they struggle to actualize worthy ideas into realities.

I have no idea how the creative process works. I only know that if I show up, most days a miracle will occur. My role in this process is solely to cooperate with the mysterious flow and strive to follow guidance I am given. Some days I fail utterly.

But some days are glorious, and even though I am only a small bit player in the whole process, I love it. because I know that, for some reason, the great Creator has endowed us with the power to allow the creative process to work, or to stop it cold by simply not showing up.

Showing up is an important victory for me.

"Life is difficult, and I believe has many conflicts in it, many challenges. But it seems to me that without those life wouldn't be interesting. The interest, the joy, the creativity, that comes from these is -- say, in Beethoven's symphonies: "Joyful, joyful, we adore thee." That's the end of the Ninth Symphony, and that "Joyful, joyful" comes only after the agony that is shown in the first part of that symphony. Now, I believe in life, and I believe in the joy of human existence, but these things cannot be experienced except as we also face the despair, also face the anxiety that every human being has to face if he lives with any creativity at all. "

- Rollo May

Demystifying Creativity

While it is easy to get caught up in the mechanics of creativity, it's important not to overanalyze it, and to stay out the way of the flow of ideas. Self-consciousness can create an awareness level that is too close to the inner critic.

The trick is to get started and JUST DO IT.

Don't think about what is is, how it works, or even why. Simply get into the flow of ideas. The best way to do this is to work at your writing each day.

Many writers choose a quiet workspace for their desk, without distractions such as email or ringing phones, and set aside a time period where they can work without outside stimuli.

For many writers, this time is first thing in the morning, after or during coffee, when the mind is fresh and even still distancing itself from the dream state.

Others are night owls and choose to write late at night into the early morning hours, when their own particular body clock seems to favor creative thought, while the rest of the world sleeps.

Even if you have no ideas, simply sitting there and free-associating with words or using tools such as tarot cards can get you into the flow of ideas and spark the creative muse.

Don't question the process – simply dive in and get into it, immersing yourself in the flow.

Writer Procrastination

We briefly explored the psychological reasons for putting off the act of writing or even thinking about ideas. A good bit of it is mental laziness and the avoidance of anxiety.

Many see the act of writing and the creative process as analogous to the Myth of Sisyphus.
Sisyphus was a figure of Greek mythology who was condemned to repeat forever the same meaningless task of pushing a boulder up a mountain, only to see it roll down again.

But remember there is joy in the effort, if we can recognize it. The act of moving forward, the act of creation is in itself the reward.
One scholar noted in an essay about the hard creative work of writing and the satisfaction to follow that "The struggle itself...is enough to fill a man's heart. One must imagine Sisyphus happy."

When you are finished this book, don't put off the act of writing by buying other books on writing.

(Ok, order them if you must, but make a pact with your self you will write every morning for one hour before you open another book!).

It's simply too easy otherwise to put off your writing until you read yet another book on writing, and though you may reason that the next book is necessary before starting, in the end realize it is your mind playing tricks on you again - it's the avoidance of pain!

I know this from first hand experience. Every writing project I undertake (including this book) goes through the same maddening cycle. Here's a typical cycle for me:

Research. Read. Research some more. Read. Buy more books on the subject. Get on the internet. Rent some documentaries. Watch TV on any subject related to X. Maybe interview some people and locate their long lost relatives. Then maybe do some genealogy and travel to the countries of their origins and perhaps undertake some archeological digs.

It's absolutely nuts.

This goes on for months before you realize that it never ends unless you end it and get down to the task of writing, and even then it can sometimes seem like herding cats or fishing for crab on the Bering Sea.

Your mind will reason "well I need this new information to make my writing better." But you'll never come to the end of this cycle unless you jump in now, because there really is no end to research.

While the writing process requires hard work, determination and anxiety, it's also intensely rewarding. Enjoy the process! In fact, the more you can get behind the joy of creating as you are doing it, the more fun the experience will be, and more you will look forward to doing it.

If you look on writing as drudgery, you will meet with even more resistance from your subconscious mind to avoid it.

Understand that your mind will take the path of least resistance until it is able to become immersed in the task, and then to be fully driven forward by the spark of inspiration.

When asked how he goes about the task of writing, Phillip Rosenthal, the creator and head writer of the successful sitcom, "Everybody Loves Raymond," said:

"I put off writing for as long as possible. I agonize over it. Mostly I worry. I worry about everything. From the idea to the possible end result of that idea – with my worst fear of failure taking center stage. Beneath that worry, even after all the success I've had, is 'this is the one. This is the idea that's going to reveal to the world I'm a fake, that I'm no good.'

While we must remember Phil is the embodiment of angst and says some of this tongue in cheek (we assume), it's our way of pointing out that it's perfectly natural to put off the act of writing and to worry.

This is a perfect example of the inner critic at work, the demon of insecurity that will strike and debilitate if you let it. Simply let go of the anxiety, let the words and ideas flow – leave the inner critic behind and get into the river's current.

Your challenge is to circumvent the natural tendency to procrastinate and to jump into the task as quickly as possible, to avoid the conscious or even unconscious avoidance behaviors that exist in us all.

2
The Creative Unconscious Examined

What is the creative unconscious? How does it work? How can I tap into it and make it work for me?

What Is It and How To Use It

The term "Unconscious" is used interchangeably with "Subconscious" or "Preconscious," defined to mean the activity of the brain which hidden from our everyday thinking awareness.

It is a scientific fact that the subconscious mind contains a vast body of knowledge, instincts, memories and ideas that, during our normal waking states of awareness, is not accessible to our conscious mind.

While we are sleeping, our subconscious mind takes over, and dreaming is the result. While we are awake, often we will see glimpses or flashes of inspirations or ideas that seem to "spring from nowhere."

That "nowhere" is the subconscious mind.

But what exactly do we mean by "conscious" and "unconscious"? The epochal influence of Freudian psychology in the early 20th century made psychoanalytical terminology a regular part of common public discourse even as the popular meanings of such terms were watered down, sometimes to the point of rendering them virtually meaningless.

A reflexive certainty that we already know what's entailed by "conscious" and "unconscious" can stand in the way of learning something useful. As Alexander Pope remarked, "Some people will never learn anything, for this reason, because they understand everything too soon."

The conscious mind, in the simplest possible terms, is what you mean when you say "I." The psychoanalytic term for it, which also happens to be the term adopted by various nondual spiritual teachers (e.g., Eckhart Tolle), which is also the term I'll regularly use here, is the ego.

The ego or "I" is your wakefulness, your awareness, your subjectivity, the mental space in which you're aware of your own thoughts and emotions and the external world around you. When you engage in rational thought, that's the conscious mind. When you perceive the sights and sounds around you, that's the conscious mind. When you recall a memory, you do so in the conscious mind. When you feel an emotion, you feel it in the conscious mind.

To call the conscious mind the ego or "I"-self is to express a crucial truth about it, namely, that we're apparently hardwired to feel that the boundary of our conscious mind is the boundary of who and what we are. In the course of growing up you learn to make the distinction between "in here" — the space of your conscious mind — and "out there" — the world you perceive as external. (Tangentially, you might note the interesting fact that your physical body occupies the second category.) From then on, you conceive and perceive yourself as a subjective presence in an external environment that is "not you," an environment that acts upon you, and upon which you can act. This is all common knowledge.

What's less readily acknowledged by many of us, even in our supposedly hip and intellectually enlightened age, is that the boundary that has been erected between "me" and "not me" by the time each of us achieves a recognizable personality in childhood also extends into the mind itself. The ego self that you sense as your sole identity is confronted by something that it perceives as other, as "not me," not only externally but internally — from behind, so to speak — in the form of the unconscious mind.

This can't be stressed too strongly. We all "know," as a matter of pop psychological wisdom, that we have an unconscious mind. It's the stuff of TV sitcoms and self-help books. But the penetrating reality of it is something much more profound, because in a very real sense it's just as true to say that your unconscious mind has you. A major portion of your full identity lies outside your conscious grasp. "You" don't stop at the boundary of your conscious sense of self.

Your unconscious is "mind stuff," a portion of your mental self or psyche, that has been walled off from who you feel yourself to be, and that now feels rather like an alien presence. Forget the quaint amusements of Freudian slips and all that. This is a revolutionary revelation on a deep life level. Your unconscious is "mind stuff," a portion of your mental self or psyche, that has been walled off from who you feel yourself to be, and that now feels rather like an alien presence. Only its alienness is far more singular and uncanny than that of the external world, for it is an inner alienness, a sense of otherness within your very self. How many presences are looking out from behind your eyes right now? Answer: at least two.

The more you dwell on it, the more bizarre and unsettling it seems. And yet it's a foundational fact of human selfhood.

The term subconscious is used in many different contexts and has no single or precise definition. This greatly limits its significance as a definition-bearing concept, and in consequence the word tends to be avoided in academic and scientific settings.

In everyday speech and popular writing, however, the term is very commonly encountered as a layperson's replacement for the unconscious mind, which in Freud's opinion is a repository for socially unacceptable ideas, wishes or desires, traumatic memories, and painful emotions put out of mind by the mechanism of psychological repression.

However, the contents do not necessarily have to be solely negative. In the psychoanalytic view, the unconscious is a force that can only be recognized by its effects — it expresses itself in the symptom.

Unconscious thoughts are not directly accessible to ordinary introspection, but can be "tapped" during the creative process and "interpreted" by special methods and techniques such as meditation, random association, dream analysis, and verbal slips (commonly known as a Freudian slip), examined and conducted during psychoanalysis.

Carl Jung developed the concept further. He divided the unconscious into two parts: the personal unconscious and the collective unconscious. The personal unconscious is a reservoir of material that was once conscious but has been forgotten or suppressed.

The idea of the "subconscious" as a powerful or potent agency has allowed the term to become prominent in the New Age and self-help literature, in which investigating or controlling its supposed knowledge or power is seen as advantageous.

In the New Age community, techniques such as autosuggestion and affirmations are believed to harness the power of the subconscious to influence a person's life and real-world outcomes, even curing sickness.

Skeptical Inquirer magazine criticized the lack of falsifiability and testability of these claims. Physicist Ali Alousi, for instance, criticized it as immeasurable and questioned the likelihood that thoughts can affect anything outside the head.

In addition, critics have asserted that the evidence provided is usually anecdotal and that, because of the self-selecting nature of the positive reports, as well as the subjective nature of any results, these reports are susceptible to confirmation bias and selection bias.

The word "subconscious" is an anglicized version of the French subconscient as coined by the psychologist Pierre Janet. Janet himself saw the subconscient as active in hypnotic suggestion and as an area of the psyche to which ideas would be consigned through a process that involved a "splitting" of the mind and a restriction of the field of consciousness.

Whether you subscribe to the belief of its origins or effectiveness, the subconscious mind remains a valuable resource of ideas that can help us in our quest to tap the wellspring of the imagination.

Brain Waves and States of Awareness

In 1924, Hans Berger, one of the greatest German scientists of the last century, was the first to revolutionize Electroencephalogram (EEG) or brain-wave tests. These tests managed to capture the very tiny voltage-fluctuations from the human brain. This is defined by the wave pattern called the frequency.

Researches have found that the human brain usually operates at 'Beta wave' state at around 14Hz and above. This is at our conscious state with active concentration.

As for subconscious mind, it becomes dominant when the brain wave is slowing down through three frequency ranges:

ALPHA WAVES - Around 7Hz to 14Hz:

This wave exists when people are usually at rest and relaxing, or meditating; scientists usually associate this state to creativity and "genius spark" moments. People who are able to tap into this state can access the wealth of creativity that lies just below the conscious awareness.

Many geniuses have been known to indulge in such states; i.e. Albert Einstein was well known to take many rest and afternoon naps in between his many important works, during which scientists believed he was tapping into this "genius spark" state.

Thus, some scientists believe that genius is not simply genetic, but is the result of a brain that has been nurtured and trained to work at Alpha and Theta stage.

Thomas Edison was a prolific inventor, shameless self-promoter, and masterful catnapper. Legend has it that he would sleep in his chair, pondering a particular problem, holding ball bearings in the palms of his hands.

After an appropriate number minutes, he'd relax enough to drop the balls, waking himself up. Then he'd go back to inventing, invigorated by the ideas or problem-solving generated by being in the relaxed state.

THETA WAVES - Around 4Hz to 7Hz
This is considered the first stage of sleep mode. This activates the gateway receptive to information beyond the usual normal state of awareness. Thus, Theta waves have also been identified as the "gateway" to learning, creativity and superb memory.

Often those who practice meditation experience this blissful state, and it has been linked to accelerated learning.

DELTA WAVES - 0.5Hz to 4Hz.
Delta waves exist only in deep sleep. Creativity and intuition are further strengthened. Sometimes, people can remember their past dreams vividly or long lost memories in this state as the subconscious brain is working actively without any external interference.

It is reported that five to fifteen minutes in Theta state can usually restore mental fatigue.

As the brainwave patterns transition from Beta to Alpha to Theta to Delta, it is reported that the human brain corresponds in synchronization, which means that the whole brain is in full harmony.

Creativity is stimulated by the slowing down of brainwave frequencies; and these are the moments that enlighten genius.

We can use these states to enlighten our creativity by relaxing into states of awareness which stimulate creativity and tap the subconscious mind.

The Two Selves

You are psychologically divided into two selves, the conscious and unconscious minds, but you feel yourself to be only the conscious part — a statement that's basically a tautology, since to feel implies to feel consciously — and this means your inner life is characterized by a strange doubleness.

Simply as a given, as a brute fact of irreducible psychological reality, you carry around with you the sense of being accompanied by an external presence that resides "behind" your conscious thoughts and sense of self.

Once you have a grasp on this fairly wondrous, bizarre, and universal situation, the natural question that arises is the concrete and ever-popular, "Now what?" What do we as writers actually do with this insight? How do we put it to practical and productive use?

The answer is found in the very nature of the differences between the dual aspects of your psyche. Each of these aspects works in its own way, and each has a proper and crucial role to play in the creative process. We put our knowledge of the psyche to practical use by learning and capitalizing on these roles.

The Demon Muse

In a nutshell, the unconscious mind supplies the content of what we write, while the ego, the voluntary conscious self, channels and shapes this unconscious material. In an even smaller nutshell — and to quote a famous pronouncement by the poet Stanley Kunitz — "the unconscious creates, the ego edits."

The ideas that you work with, the chains of thought and impression that appear in your mind as if from nowhere and seem to take on a life of their own as you race to record and refine them — these all carry that perceived quality of independence and spontaneity precisely because they're emerging into consciousness from your unconscious mind. When you enter this "inspired" state, you are literally engaged in a psychologically collaborative effort between your two selves.

Getting to know this aspect of yourself is getting to know the permanent visitor in your psyche and the deep life pattern it wants to actualize through you. So this is all to say that for purposes of developing a working psychology of creativity, we can equate the unconscious mind with both the muse and the daimon. In Western history the muse is the classical symbol of creative inspiration.

The word "inspiration" in its root sense connotes a state of being filled with a divine presence ("in" + "spire" means both the act of physical inhalation and the act of infusing someone with spirit). The daimon is the keeper of a person's deep character, life pattern, and destiny"

Pairing the two figures yields the idea of the demon muse, the spirit that inspires a person to do the work for which he or she is uniquely gifted and intended. Getting to know this aspect of yourself is getting to know the permanent visitor in your psyche and the deep life pattern it wants to actualize through you.

One of the most powerful acts you can take to develop a rich creative life is to deliberately give up conscious control over the ultimate shape, nature, and direction of your work.

Hand over the responsibility for those things to your deep self, your unconscious mind, your demon muse, and recognize that your role as ego is simply to midwife and refine the material that wants to be written.

The Universal Mind

Many sages and scribes have speculated on the existence of the "Universal Mind." The theory is that there is a vast body of knowledge that exists out there in the universe which can be tapped, which may explain why there are so many common ideas.

It's been called various things. Edgar Cayce, the Sleeping Prophet who had an uncanny ability to tap into states of the subconscious mind, called it the Akashic Records.

Carl Jung, the famed psychologist, wrote extensively on the theory, and called it the Creative Unconscious.

Ernest Holmes, who founded the Science of Mind religion, called it "Universal Mind, the center of all intelligence."

Whether the universal mind exists, or whether our ideas exist independently within our own unconscious minds, the important point to remember is that there does exist beneath the surface an entire universe of ideas, thoughts and shared experiences.

Some believe, as Jung did, (and later explored extensively by Joseph Campbell,) that these many thoughts and shared experiences are represented through symbols and myths called archetypes.

Jung said:

"Many artists, philosophers, and even scientists owe some of their best ideas to inspirations . . . from the unconscious - The ability to reach a rich vein of such material, and to translate it effectively . . . is commonly called genius - We can find clear proof of this fact in the history of science itself. The so-called "mystical" experience of the French philosopher Descartes involved a . . . sudden revelation in which he saw in a flash the "order of all sciences".

The British author Robert Louis Stevenson had spent years looking for a story that would fit his "strong sense of man's double being," when the plot of Dr. Jekyll and Mr. Hyde was suddenly revealed to him in a dream.

Joseph Campbell, quoted from his wonderful work on myths, heroes and the hero's journey:

"Willed introversion, in fact, is one of the classic implements of creative genius and can be employed as a deliberate device. It drives the psychic energies into depth and activates the lost continent of unconscious infantile and archetypal images. The result, of course, may be a disintegration of consciousness more or less complete (neurosis, psychosis: the plight of the spellbound Daphne); but on the other hand, if the personality is able to absorb and integrate the new forces, there will be experienced an almost super-human degree of self-consciousness and masterful control.

This is a basic principle of the Indian disciplines of yoga. It has been the way, also, of many creative spirits in the West. It cannot be described, quite, as an answer to any specific call. Rather, it is a deliberate, terrific refusal to respond to anything but the deepest, highest, richest answer to the as yet unknown demand of some waiting void within: a kind of total strike, or rejection of the offered terms of life, as a result of which some power of transformation carries the problem to a plane of new magnitudes, where it is suddenly and finally resolved."

There are also many levels and modes of perception of reality. Many times these moods and modes can be triggered by dreams, watching movies, reading books, or simply changing ones environment, whether for a few moments or for a few days or weeks.

These various moods are the thing we are trying to invoke in readers, to take them away into a new dimension. We must first go to those places in the imagination ourselves before we can set them down to paper to transport the reader.

Creativity: Innate Or Learned?

A study by George Land reveals that we are naturally creative and as we grow up we learn to be uncreative. Creativity is a skill that can be developed and a process that can be managed.
Learning to be creative is akin to learning a sport. It requires practice to develop the right muscles, and a supportive environment in which to flourish. Business leaders are increasingly adopting the principles and practices of art and design to help build creative muscle in their organizations.

Beliefs that only special, talented people are creative-and you have to be born that way-diminish our confidence in our creative abilities.

The notion that geniuses such as Shakespeare, Picasso and Mozart were 'gifted' is a myth, according to a study at Exeter University.

Researchers examined outstanding performances in the arts, mathematics and sports, to find out if "the widespread belief that to reach high levels of ability a person must possess an innate potential called talent."

The study concludes that excellence is determined by:
☐ opportunities
☐ encouragement
☐ training
☐ motivation
☐ & most of all-practice

Few showed early signs of promise prior to parental encouragement.

No one reached high levels of achievement in their field without devoting thousands of hours of serious training. Mozart trained for 16 years before he produced an acknowledged master work. Moreover many high performers achieve levels of excellence today that match the capabilities of a Mozart, or a Gold Medalist from the turn of the century.

Writers know that by working at their craft each day, immersing themselves in the process, and relaxing and sleeping with their ideas provides a perfect breeding ground for creativity to flourish.

In a CBS News poll of 1,048 randomly chosen adults surveyed nationwide, more than half (53%) of the respondents said that creativity is something a person has to be born with.

Approximately one third (35%) said creativity is something that can be taught. The views were nearly the same across all demographic groups. Surprisingly, this poll reveals that more people think that creativity is innate but, with practice, the creativity muscle can be developed.

Author and creativity expert Daniel Pink in the CBS News website article, "The Wellspring of American Creativity," believes that all people have at least some creative potential simply because they are human. He explains that he doesn't think everybody is a budding Picasso, Edison or Toni Morrison, but human beings are defined by their ability to create.

Pink also says that creativity is the ability to give the world something it didn't know it was missing. He gives the example of the iPod and how tens of millions of people who now carry one didn't know that they were missing it eight years ago. He credits America with being a nurturing country where failure is less stigmatized than other countries, giving way for people to take more creative risks.

Building the Creative Muscle

Routine and habit squash creative ideas and thoughts and can stifle a person. Once a person becomes stifled, the mind is not challenged. When people think creatively, new realms of possibility open up where ideas and thoughts are born. But to keep creativity in the forefront it must be practiced. Here are some way to practice creativity and get the juices flowing:

- Exercise the creative mind – Take photos, draw pictures, have an unusual conversation, take a different route, try a new recipe - whatever it is approach it with a new perspective and zest, this alone can unleash creativity.
- Read books other than the usual – People tend to stick with what they like. If a person only reads non-fiction books then he or she can be missing out on other inspiring books.
- Design an environment conducive to creativity – Create an environment where creativity can flourish. People are most inspired when they surround themselves with the things they love such as photographs, artwork, decorations, certain color schemes, and so on.

- Use mind maps – Mind mapping is a creative tool that visually connects things, ideas, and facts, just as the mind works. They can be used for creative problem-solving, decision-making, project planning, and brainstorming ideas. Here is a sample of what one looks like from the website, Livethesolution.com.
- Write, write and then write some more – Writing can uncover ideas buried in the subconscious so write about anything, just write, and do it daily.
- Commune with nature – Taking a walk outside in the woods, by the water, or simply around the neighborhood can clear the mind and lay the groundwork for a creative endeavor.
- Think out of the box – To children, creativity comes naturally. They act out plays, create shows and play dress-up. Think out of the box and do something out of the ordinary everyday.
- Explore your fantasies and get out of the comfort zone – If there is something that a person thinks about doing such as going up in a hot air balloon, deep sea diving or signing up for a cooking class perhaps it's time to try it out. When people take themselves out of their comfort zones and engage in their fantasies, not letting fear stop them, they grow, expand, and life opens up.

Creative Life Imagining

When Michelangelo described how his Statue of David was created he said, "I saw the angel in the marble and carved until I set him free." Michelangelo, through his mental imagery, birthed a genius creation.

Visualization or imagination is the source for all that is created, so the more people visualize something they want to create, the more likely it will get created. Henry David Thoreau said, "The world is but a canvas to the imagination." To live a creative life, start to imagine things such as what is desired in life, what life will look like when goals and dreams are reached, and how it will feel. Visualizing has a powerful effect on the subconscious and will move desires into reality.

"A rock pile ceases to be a rock pile the moment a single man contemplates it, bearing within him the image of a cathedral."
~Antoine de Saint-Exupery

The Law of Physics In Creativity

The basic law of physics is that what is in motion tends to stay in motion. The opposite of this is that what is not in motion tends to stay that way, like sitting on the couch watching Wheel of Fortune waiting for inspiration to strike.

So once you've primed the pump and the ideas are flowing, stay with it, get the words out on to the paper and try to keep the momentum going while the atoms of creativity are in motion.

Any experience we have is a result of a flow of energy. Without a flow of energy nothing moves. If nothing moves, there is nothing to experience. To understand how Creation works and we have the experiences we do we need to understand energy and how it flows to create the experiences we have.

Originally, Physics by definition, and simply said, was defined as the study of the nature and properties of matter an energy. However, we now know matter is just a form of energy and one can be converted into the other.
As a result, we can now say Physics is the study of the nature and properties of energy of which matter is only one form of energy.

In the study of Physics, it has been found there are concepts, principles, "rules" and "laws" which govern the various forms of energy and, of course, there are still many more to uncover. In understanding what has been uncovered, we can transform, and have transformed, the world in which we live.

In fact, we now have the understanding and ability to completely destroy human life if we so choose to do so. As such, there are applications of what we have learned that are considered constructive and beneficial to individual and/or humanity and there are applications that are consider destructive. The choice of how we use what we have learned is our choice.

The laws and rules themselves do not change as a result of how they are applied or where they are applied. Also, they can be applied equally well by any individual who understands them regardless of the sex, race, creed, national origins, and any other way we like to differentiate one human from another.

Similarly, there are no secrets.

They can be uncovered by anyone who is observant and willing to do the necessary experiments.

In the exploration of our creativity, it was found there are similar concepts, principles, rules and laws that govern how we create our experiences and the reality we experience. These too can be applied constructively and beneficial to the individual and/or humanity and there are applications that are consider destructive.

The choice of how we use what we learn is our choice. These creativity laws and rules themselves do not change as a result of how they are applied or where they are applied. Also, they can be applied equally well by any individual who understands them regardless of the sex, race, creed, national origins, and any other way we like to differentiate one human from another. Similarly, there are no secrets. They can be uncovered by anyone who is observant and willing to do the necessary experiments.

Anxiety And Fear: The Fuel Of Creativity

If we are open to feeling, what we will discover is there is anxiety within the creative/creation process. It arises from two basic reasons.

One is that since energy can neither be created or destroyed some of the existing world must be destroyed and sacrificed to both free the energy and create the space for the new creation. The destruction of parts of the existing world is experienced as chaos. Chaos in the creative/creation process is inescapable.

The second reason is that creativity by its very nature takes us into the unknown. One of the most important things to realize about creativity is that mind only knows the past. To create means to bring into existence something not previously experienced or significantly different from the past. Consequently, mind is ill equipped to face the unknown. Mind will characterize whatever it perceives, including the energy giving rise to the thoughts we have, based on the experiences it has had.

This means that any thought we have is not necessarily accurate. The more what experience is like the past, the more our mind properly characterizes what we experience. However, the more what we experience is not like the past, the more inaccurate our mind becomes at characterizing what we experience.

Anything mind thinks about what needs to be done in a creative endeavor and/or it provides as a characterization of the energy we feel leading us into creative endeavors will be inaccurate. Mind is aware of this fact and will be anxious about it for it loses control in a creative endeavor.

Our mind may panic and feel frightened at the prospect of the internal changes it is experience or the external change it see occurring, or we may feel some anxiety at the destruction which is occurring.

Overlay with the unknown the chaos of creation, the multidimensional aspects of Creation and our being, the accompanying destructions of the known all of one's worst fears can be projected into, or onto, our creative endeavor.

Any transition from an old way to a new way has this element of chaos and any chaotic situation always brings a certain level of anxiety if not outright fear.

In this regard, the anxiety of creation always fuels an fear of the unknown. It takes courage and strength of will to hold to an intention and to not doubt when mind has no way to fully understand what is happening.

Since we are multidimensional beings and the creative/creation process is occurring on multiple levels at different rates and at different points in the process, there are periods if not a general feeling of anxiety we may find in our life. If we have not numbed what we feel there is always something we can feel anxious about and something to feel joyful about. However, many of us tend to focus on the joyful and try and avoid the anxiety not realizing the both are part of the same cycle of creation.

As a result we approach life in a rather unbalanced way. We see that which makes us feel good and try and avoid that which makes us feel bad. In the end we creatively limit our options and continually repeat the past for we are unwilling fact the anxiety of creation to bring into existence that which we have not yet experience.

We do not enter the unknown because of the fear the pain we may create yet, in doing so, we deny the pleasures and joy we can find. Rather then journey into the unknown and face our fears and potential painful experiences, we seek a valley of contentment were we can be assured all if fine.

In understanding the creative/creation process for what it is and the cyclic nature of pain and pleasure, we can find great solitude in the realization what we experience is only consciousness at play with itself. We need not be pulled into the drama. We can take the perspective of the detached witness.

This awareness can help create an inner satisfaction that never runs dry no matter what is happening in the world. It is this awareness which allows one to freely surrender to what is occurring and flow with the events as they unfold for they see the creation process for what it is.

Although there is the possibility of experiencing the anxiety of creation in the creative/creation process, one can become a detached witness to remain in a place of calmness during the creative/creation process.

"Joy is the zest that you get out of using your talents, your understanding, the totality of your being, for great aims. Musicians, men who wrote music -- Mozart and Beethoven and the rest of them -- they always showed considerable anxiety, because they were in the process of loving beauty, of feeling joy when they heard a beautiful combination of notes. That's the kind of feeling that goes with creativity. That's why I say the courage to create. Creation does not come out of simply what you're born with. That must be united with your courage, both of which cause anxiety but also great joy. "

- Rollo May

Is Tapping The Creative Unconscious Dangerous?

Some may fear themselves in danger of going into a state of neuroses or psychosis when attempting to mine the depths of the unconscious mind. While it is true that there are some among us who might experience uncomfortable or anxious feelings when exploring "the depths of the soul" as it were, it need not concern you.

When one considers the millions of artistic people who daily exercise their creative abilities without incident, it appears that tapping into one's creative wellspring bears minimal risk of psychic disintegration.

Although there have been many artists over the years who descended into an abyss of mental deterioration; (Van Gogh was one such example), it might very well be these individuals may have developed psychosis or neuroses whether or not they engaged in the creative endeavor.

3
Developing Your Creative Unconscious

Keeping and Feeding of the Muse

As for exactly how to accomplish this feat of self-knowledge in which you decide to let your work be driven by your creative unconscious, is an excellent first step. One of Ray Bradbury's own writing gurus stated the matter with exquisite clarity in her masterwork about the training of authorial genius:

"It is possible to train both sides of the character to work in harmony, and the first step in that education is to consider that you must teach yourself not as though you were one person, but two. . . . By isolating as far as possible the functions of these two sides of the mind, even by considering them not merely as aspects of the same mind but as separate personalities, we can arrive at a kind of working metaphor, impossible to confuse with reality, but infinitely helpful in self-education. . . . If you are to write well you must come to terms with the enormous and powerful part of your nature which lies behind the threshold of immediate knowledge."
– Dorothea Brande, Becoming a Writer (1934)

As a useful experiment, you might consider paying attention to your own mind and the interplay of conscious awareness with unconscious processes, since you have to learn the difference between them before you can take action to train them.

Whenever memories pop up from nowhere, thoughts and ideas take off on wild and spontaneous tangents, and/or you find yourself helplessly fascinated by a person, idea, scene, situation, or circumstance, you're probably experiencing the interplay of your two natures. You-as-ego are receiving deliveries from the unconscious mind, which are recognizable as such by the fact of their psychologically involuntary character.

These deliveries are in turn the product of your unconscious mind's interpretive and transformative action upon the things you have encountered and experienced in the world around you. This same synergistic process is the root of all authentic creativity. Learn the deep workings of your own mind, and you learn the key to cooperating with psychological reality and thereby realizing (making real) what's wanting to be said through you.

"In a lifetime, we stuff ourselves with sounds, sights, smells, tastes, and textures of people, animals, landscapes, events, large and small. We stuff ourselves with these impressions and experiences and our reaction to them. Into our subconscious go not only factual data but reactive data, our movement toward or away from the sensed events.

These are the stuffs, the foods, on which The Muse grows. This is the storehouse, the file. . . . What is The Subconscious to every other man, in its creative aspect becomes, for writers, The Muse. They are two names for one thing. . . . Here is the stuff of originality. For it is in the totality of experience reckoned with, filed, and forgotten, that each man is truly different from all others in the world."

– *Ray Bradbury - "How to Keep and Feed a Muse," in* Zen in the Art of Writing: Releasing the Creative Genius within You *(1992)*

Tapping Your Creative Unconscious

"I'm a great believer in the power of unconscious. We sit down with a blank page and it's a spectacular moment to sit there and have the audacity to think that you can create something that other people are going to relate to" - Paul Williams - Composer

Since the unconscious by its very nature is something we are not aware of much of the time, we must find innovative ways to plumb the depths. A good analogy might be fishing. We are floating in a boat on the surface of a great lake, (our conscious waking state) and the unconscious lies beneath the surface, where ideas swim below us.

We must cast the line and fish – although we cannot see what exists just below the calm surface.

Since we know a lot of the work that gets done in the unconscious mind works behind the scenes and is stimulated into action by the work we do in our waking states, we must first give the unconscious mind the raw data it needs to do its work for us.

That means we must undertake our writing project with gusto each and every day, toiling away at the hard work of writing. As we participate consciously in the creative process, working at the daily task of writing, the unconscious mind is doing its own work, much like the second unit on a film shoot.

You will find that during your rest periods from such activity, when you have taken the mind off of a particular task, and while doing some unrelated task or mundane activity or even recreational distraction, ideas will flow to the surface. Much like fishing, it's a hit and miss proposition. But rest assured, as you do this process on a daily basis, the ideas will come.

Another way to tap into the creative unconscious is during sleep and dreaming, which we will cover in a later section One tried and true technique for discovering your unconscious mind in its uniqueness and particularity is to engage in the regular practice of morning writing.
This means something quite specific; it's more than just sitting down to ramble on paper over a light breakfast..

The trick with this technique is to have everything ready — pen and paper laid out if you're going to write by hand, typewriter or computer standing ready if you're planning to type — and then to get up a little earlier than normal and head straight to your writing station, where you immediately and unreflectively start writing.

You write absolutely anything that comes to mind. A memory of last night's dream, if one is present. Thoughts about what you'll be doing that day. A rehashing of some event from the previous day. A nursery rhyme. Complaints about how tired you are and how you'd rather be lying in bed.

A stream-of-consciousness flow of relative nonsense. In other words, absolutely anything that arises in your mindspace. Keep doing this for ten minutes.

Over time, gradually build up to longer sessions. When you do this correctly, you effectively tap into your unconscious mind before your ego has had a chance to wake up completely. Your normal mental defenses and filters are down. Things just come out that you're later shocked to find you've written.

You would never collaborate with another person on any project without first gauging your respective goals and temperaments. The same reasoning applies directly to the process of artistic creation, except the collaborative relationship in this case is an inner one between you and your creative unconscious.

This element of revelatory self-discovery is, naturally, the whole point. It's built into the very nature of the exercise, but you'll need to commit to the practice for it to work. Make at least a two-week commitment, and preferably a longer one.

A month is good.

Solemnly vow not to reread what you've written until the whole period is over. Then let your work cool off for another week after that. If you do this, when you finally pick your work up and read back over it, you'll be astonished at the things you wrote with absolutely no memory of having done so, and/or you'll be struck by the significance of things that didn't seem all that striking when you wrote them.

Yes, you'll have to wade through a lot of muddy junk to find the diamonds, and you'll cringe at a few things here and there. But the upside will far outweigh the downside.

If you will deliberately look at these writings with a critical and objective eye, as if they were written by somebody else whose personality and passions, interests and abilities, voice and style you're trying to discover, you'll make great headway in finding out the native bent of your inner genius.

Be advised that Dorothea Brande's Becoming a Writer and Julia Cameron's The Artist's Way contain wonderfully detailed instructions for using this technique. Brande includes particularly valuable information on extending the exercise into the daylight hours, so that you coax your unconscious to speak freely at any time, not just in the early morning.

For that matter, Natalie Goldberg in her modern classic Writing Down the Bones: Freeing the

Writer Within offers all kinds of useful advice, both practical and attitudinal, for coaxing a free flow of words from the unconscious in all sorts of circumstances and surroundings.

The second technique: a dialogue between your ego and unconscious mind.

This one is more of a direct attempt to personify your genius by giving it a voice and interacting with it as a separate entity. You must begin to make a conscious acquaintance with what lies within.

One way to begin is to compose a completely spontaneous dialogue between your conscious self ("I") and your unconscious (give it a separate identity and name, or let one emerge from the dialogue).

When you finish your dialogue, describe the personalities of the two speakers. What kind of person is the "I"? What kind of person is the unconscious? (Individuals are highly variable; you may find creatures other than topdogs and underdogs.).

Are they opposites or are they kindred spirits? Are they at loggerheads, or do they achieve resolution? (Don't try to force a resolution; that is your ego taking charge. Be absolutely honest about where you are at this moment.)

The kinship between this technique and the first should be obvious. In both cases you are trying to divine the peculiar character of your unconscious mind by letting it speak on paper, but in the first you do so by writing at a time when the ego is relatively subdued, so that the unconscious can speak through you with little interference, while in the second you deliberately inhabit your fully-awake ego space and generate the sense of talking with your unconscious as an outside entity.

I can tell you from having practiced both techniques numerous times that both of them really do work. Both can yield crucial information about yourself, information that is relevant not just to your life as a writer or artist but to your life in general.

Both are equivalent to self-psychotherapy, since the primary goal of all forms of psychotherapy, regardless of their specific schools, is to achieve a harmonious relationship between the conscious and unconscious minds by airing the contents of the unconscious.

It's axiomatic that whatever is unconscious has the power to dominate you in ways you cannot and do not recognize. Establishing a clear channel of self-aware exchange between your two selves reduced the unconscious mind's demonic-daimonic potential to induce possessed-type behavior in the form of violently uncontrollable fantasies and impulses.

You may well want to be a violently impulsive writer, somebody who creates in accord with Wordworth's dictum that poetry is "emotion recollected in tranquility" and then manages through his writing to discharge and recreate that original flaming emotion within the reader.

Think of yourself in your conscious aspect as a kind of conduit or channel for the unconscious energies that are wanting to come through you.

In coming to know your unconscious mind, your daimon, your personal genius, you are unblocking the channel by learning to step aside and lightly direct and shape the torrent as it flows into the world.

Getting Into The Zone

Much of getting into the zone is through the process of *immersion*.

Once you are immersed in the process of creating a work, once you have cleared the distractions away and the inhibitions, the ideas will flow as the work becomes an integral part of your focus.

There are several schools of though as to whether you are fishing from within for ideas, or reaching out to some external source in the universe which you are tapping into.

Some feel the latter model allows for less anxiety, since all one is doing is participating in the process – which one you subscribe to is yours uniquely.

The main thing is to JUST DO IT.

Don't procrastinate just jump in, and get the basics down on paper, you can always rewrite and reshape the material later.

Free Association

One technique to use to tap into the wellspring of the unconscious is free association. Psychologists use this method to help patients to unlodge unconscious or repressed thoughts.

Free association contains elements of several other idea-generating techniques and depends on a mental 'stream of consciousness' and network of associations of which there are two:

Serial association, start with a trigger, you record the flow of ideas that come to mind, each idea triggering the next, ultimately reaching a potentially useful one.

Centered association, (which is close to classical brainstorming) prompts you to generate multiple associations to the original trigger so that you 'delve' into a particular area of associations.

As a rule the serial mode is used to 'travel' until you find an idea that you find of some interest, you then engage the centered mode to 'delve' more deeply around the interesting item. Once you have exhausted the centered investigation, you being to 'travel' again, and so on.

Follow the intriguing and look for ideas that attract your attention as particularly strong, intriguing, surprising, etc. even if they don't seem instantly appropriate to your problem. This attraction frequently signals links to a useful set of associations, and so could possibly justify a further phase of centered free association around the 'attractive' idea.

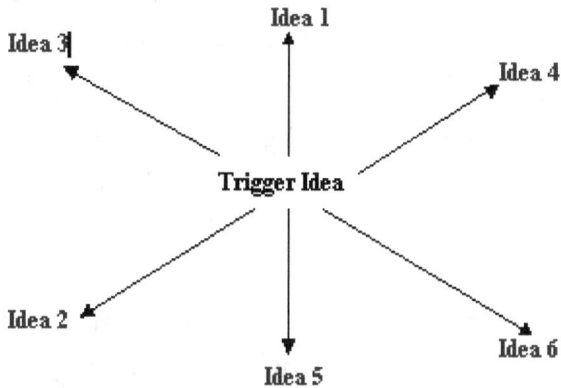

Idea 1

Idea 3

Idea 4

Trigger Idea

Idea 2

Idea 6

Idea 5

Free Writing

Free writing - (as opposed to writing for free) also known as free form, free association or stream-of-consciousness writing - can be used in order to clear the mind in preparation for meditation or as a meditative technique in itself.

With this exercise, you write down everything that enters your mind. Structure, grammar, spelling and coherence are not important.

The essential factor is to note down everything that comes to you in the moment without censorship or hesitation.

This form of writing is not meant to be poetic or wise or even to make sense. (Although if it is poetic, wise and sensible, then it's a bonus.)

Free writing, like the free association psychoanalytic method it is based on, may be awkward, angry, embarrassing, uncomfortable or it may be profound, aesthetic or humbling.

It could be mundane and ordinary and filled with trivial details. Or it could be cathartic, cleansing and exorcising. You could keep it in a special notebook, type it on your PC, or simply write it on a sheet of paper and rip it up when you have finished. Some creative writers use this technique as a warm up exercise to kick start their writing sessions.

In her book, *The Artist's Way: A Course in Discovering and Recovering Your Creative Self,* Julia Cameron teaches a similar technique to artists and writers called Morning Pages where you write three daily pages of free form writing first thing in the morning by hand.

Free form writing gives you the space to unclutter your mind and refocus your thoughts. You don't even have to read over what you have written.

Sometimes the act of writing it all out and getting it out of your head is enough. Most of the time though, it is good to read over what you have written as there could be some hidden gems, insights, ideas and solutions buried beneath your random ramblings.

Sometimes it can be interesting to look at the symbols and images that crop up in your writing and highlight or underline them noticing whether they are visual or colorful, whether they are related to sounds (auditory) or whether they are related to movement (kinesthetic).

Free writing can be used as a powerful technique to unleash your creativity and connect you with the hidden parts of your psyche and your imagination – that invisible world we call the subconscious.

Meditation

How does meditation support creativity?

Here are 3 states of mind that we can cultivate through meditation.

Each one fosters creativity:

1. Letting go of the 'me, mine, myself' mind-tape In order to do something selflessly, we need to dive completely into the action and forget ourselves in the process.
2. Being kind to ourselves - A kindly attitude allows us to experiment with failure without

our grumpy inner editor ripping us to shreds.

3. Stilling the mind A mind cluttered with thoughts lacks the spaciousness needed for creativity. It helps to be still for a few minutes before starting a creative endeavor. The easiest way to still the mind is to pay tender regard to the breath, or to listen to sounds. When we start the creative process from this point of stillness, ideas flow naturally and freely.

Stream of Consciousness Writing

Stream-of-consciousness is a narrative method of writing in which the author writes as though he is in the mind of the characters. This technique attempts at capturing the natural way of human thinking. The thoughts of humans often jump from one place to another and the author attempts to capture this phenomenon.

Stream-of-consciousness writing is usually regarded as a special form of interior monologue and is characterized by associative leaps in syntax and punctuation that can make the prose difficult to follow.

Stream of consciousness and interior monologue are distinguished from dramatic monologue, where the speaker is addressing an audience or a third person, which is used chiefly in poetry or drama. In stream of consciousness, the speaker's thought processes are more often depicted as overheard in the mind (or addressed to oneself); it is primarily a fictional device.

The term was introduced to the field of literary studies from that of psychology, where it was coined by philosopher and psychologist William James.

Many wonderful examples exist from literature, from William Burroughs's Naked Lunch to Thomas Pynchon's Gravity's Rainbow.

One of the more popular literary writers who used this technique extensively was William Faulkner.

Novices to William Faulkner's writings may find themselves confused and disconcerted while attempting to decode what appears to be nonsensical rambling throughout many of his novels.

Paragraph (if there is any) upon paragraph devoid of punctuation and erratic jumping from topic to topic are enough to drive anyone examining his works for the first time, to the safety of a Harlequin novel. Those accustomed to periods and initial caps rudely awaken to the literary concept of "stream of consciousness."

Initially, reading stream of consciousness is much like the sound of fingernails scraping across a blackboard. Years of indoctrination into grammar and punctuation send up flares of disapproval, bordering on disgust. But is this innovative method of character identification mere babble or literary genius?

Faulkner's Sound and the Fury, replete with this writing technique, has inspired critics to dismantle and analyze his characters to the point of exhaustion.

As defined by Murfin and Ray, stream of consciousness is: [A] literary technique that approximates the flow (or jumble) of thoughts and sensory impressions that pass through the mind each instant. Psychological association (rather than rules of syntax or logic) determines the presence or absence as well as the order, of elements in the "stream" [...] (456).

Faulkner manages, in his use of this technique, to put into words the fleeting of a thought through time and space, darting from one subject to another without so much as a breath in between. The reader, in turn, gains deeper insight into the emotional struggles with which the character is faced—a sort of tormented soliloquy within the deepest recesses of one's mind, not to be shared with others.

He does so through his use (or lack of) traditional punctuation and writing style. This writing style mimics the rapid and scattered nature of our thoughts, darting from topic to topic like mosquitoes to bodies on a hot, summer day. Quentin's chapter, "June Second, 1910," is perhaps the most scrutinized among critics.

Margaret D. Bauer, in her article, "'I Have Sinned in That I Have Betrayed the Innocent Blood': Quentin's Recognition of His Guilt" addresses the mental journey that resulted in Quentin's suicide: [. . .] it is the third scene in this flashback, Quentin's last extended memory of himself and Caddy before his suicide, which is the climactic moment of the section.

This recollection is particularly agonizing to Quentin because it reminds him of his own culpability regarding Caddy's destruction. Once this memory surfaces, Quentin can no longer escape the fact that for him his sister gave up a chance, however slight it may have been, of leading a "normal" life [...]. Quentin's inability to live any longer with this guilt, then, can be seen as another reason for his suicide (70).

The last seven pages of the chapter are a blur of passion and agony. Quentin has returned to his room, bloodied by the father of Caddie's baby, searching in his mind for answers to the "what ifs" in his life and the lives of his family.

"[. . .] if I'd just had a mother so I could say Mother Mother" (172). He returns to the present, dabbing the blood stains on his clothes with gasoline. Repeatedly, Quentin drifts off into thought, re-enacting in his mind scenes from his childhood in a desperate attempt to make sense of his pain.

> "...it was to isolate her out of the loud world so that it would have to flee us of necessity and the sound of it would be as though it had never been and he did you try to make her do it and i i was afraid to i was afraid she might and then it wouldn't have done any good but if i could tell you we did it would have been so and then the others wouldnt be so and then the world would roar away ".

There appears, then, to be a method to Faulkner's "madness." The experienced and determined Faulknerian can sift through the crimes against punctuation to unearth the true messages that lie deep beneath the run on sentences and erratic thought sequences. Rather than needing a quick course in Grammar 101, Faulkner has captured the movements of the mind on paper, illusive as a butterfly, yet powerfully packed with implication.

Stream of consciousness writing aims to provide a textual equivalent to the stream of a fictional character's consciousness. It creates the impression that the reader is eavesdropping on the flow of conscious experience in the character's mind, gaining intimate access to their private "thoughts".

It involves presenting in the form of written text something that is neither entirely verbal nor textual. Stream of consciousness writing was developed in the early decades of the twentieth century when writers became interested in finding ways of laying open for readers' inspection, in a way impossible in real life, the imagined inner lives of their fictional characters.

To start a stream of consciousness exercise, sit quietly in a room with nothing but a pen and paper. Put your pen to the page and start writing whatever comes to your mind. Now it doesn't matter if it makes sense, if you write in complete sentences, if you use correct grammar, complete a thought or just make noises! Just keep writing, no matter what it is that comes to your mind.

If your mind becomes totally blank, just write something like, 'my mind is blank, my mind is blank', just keep writing that until something else pops into your head. This is a good way to clear junk out of your head, you know, the day to day minutia that clouds our thinking from time to time.

Do this exercise for at least thirty minutes and save your writings in a journal. You can go back and look through your stream of consciousness exercise to glean writing ideas from them later on.

If you are having a lot of trouble with this exercise you may need to focus in on something to help you out. Pick a topic to stream on, for example, fishing, and write everything you can think of on this subject whether it be a trip with your dad when you were young or a commercial about a singing bass that hangs on your wall. Fill a page with things about fishing.

Focused stream of consciousness writing can be a great help when you are working on a project that requires more exploration of a subject. If you are so blocked that you can't even think of a topic to stream on, just turn on the television and write about the first subject you see.

Focused stream of consciousness writing can be saved in another journal and when you are working on projects that involve any of your themes, you can look to them for a little insight.

The best way to open your stream of consciousness is to just start writing and write about anything, don't worry about how good or bad it is because no one is going to read it except for you. This is your one chance to just hang loose with yourself and not worry if you have all of your I's dotted and T's crossed, have fun with it!

Creative Visualization

Research suggests that creative visualization can effectively assist people in creating positive change. In a study published in Research Quarterly,

Australian psychologist Alan Richardson found that athletes were able to improve muscle memory by visualizing certain athletic activities. Athletes who visualized making free throws on a daily basis over a period of 20 days improved just as much (24%) as athletes who physically practiced for the same amount of time.

Numerous studies have also shown creative visualization, such as guided imagery, to have positive health outcomes. Cancer patients who, in addition to medical treatment, visualize their bodies successfully destroying cancer cells have higher remission rates and life expectancies.

Creative visualization is also effective in pain-management.

In her book *Creative Visualization*, personal development guru Shakti Gawain explains, "Creative visualization is magic in the truest and highest meaning of the word. It involves understanding and aligning yourself with the natural principles that govern the workings of our into fruition.

Here are a few suggestions to try:

1. Visualize a completed manuscript. When you're at the beginning of a novel project, a completed manuscript often seems so far into the future as to be incomprehensible...but thinking of it as incomprehensible, as unlikely to materialize, is a good way of making sure that happens. So a simple visualization to start off with, and to return to, is a complete manuscript sitting on your desk. Don't just picture it in your head--though do look at it closely, at how pristine it is coming off the printer, how worn the edges get as you read through and mark it up--but imagine the tactile feel of it as you thumb the pages. Give yourself a paper cut with it. Bring it up to your "nose" and smell it. Shoo the mental cat away from it. It's not a unicorn or a yeti. It's doable and inevitable. (This is my feel-good tip, true...but this visualization has helped me immensely at times when a full three-

hundred pages seemed impossible. Or even when the next page seemed impossible.)

2. Write back jacket copy. Imagining your back jacket copy--that succinct and seductive copy that turns a browser into a buyer--can help you keep the big picture in mind, the goal you're working toward. In fact, I'd even suggest trying your hand at back jacket copy...if you had to sum up your novel in a paragraph, in such a way that lures a reader in and gets to the heart of what your novel is about, how would you capture that in just a few lines? Doing so can help you see what it is you're really trying to achieve with the work...and can help you focus the work on what's important. (Don't feel like you've made a mistake if, halfway through the book, you realize your back jacket copy has changed and that you need to tweak it...your conception of the book should change over the course of the project. It should get sharper.)

3. Keep images around that inspire the work. I tend to work outside my home, so it's not like I carry around little pictures to tape up around my computer in the coffee shop. (I do keep images related to what I'm working on taped around my home computer.) But when I'm working on a long project, I keep wallpaper on my laptop that reminds me of the world I'm trying to create,

which helps subtly inspire me or ground me in that world.

Tarot Cards

Although the tarot is most often used as a tool for divination, tarot cards are also great, practical tools for writing and creative thinking. Corrine Kenner, author of "Tarot for Writers", explains that well-known writers, such as John Steinbeck and Stephen King, have used tarot cards for inspiration. She adds that Italian novelist Italo Calvino went so far as to call the tarot "a machine for writing stories."

Tarot cards are a great tool to access the unconscious, through the use of archetypes and symbols.

If you're thinking of writing a novel, you can apply the imagery and symbolism of the 78 cards of the tarot to help you develop plot, conflict, character profiles, dialogue, and scenery, as well as to introduce unpredictable elements.

The cards can even serve as a creativity prompt if you hit a brick wall while you're writing. With a tarot deck beside you, you won't be starting out with a blank sheet of paper. Instead, you'll have a world of imagery as your disposal, which, if you allow your imagination and intuition to step forward, will begin to move, speak, and take action. This article will help you get started in using the tarot to write your novel.

Choosing a Tarot Deck

There are many different tarot decks which you can choose from, including everything from the Lord of the Rings Tarot–with "Death" depicted as Gandalf fighting the Balrog–to a Jane Austen Tarot, in which each card represents a character or scene from one of her novels. Arthur Edward Waite and Pamela Colman Smith created the best-selling Rider-Waite-Smith tarot deck in 1909, but there are many others that I feel are more contemporary and creativity oriented.

Tarot for Writers 101

You don't have to become an expert on the meaning of the tarot cards in order to use them as a creativity tool. Once you have a general idea of the symbolism of the cards, you can apply your own interpretations and use them as a springboard for your own ideas and impressions. The tarot will help you in allowing your intuition to tell you stories which you can then get down on paper. In essence, you'll be taking the open ended images on the cards and projecting a story onto them.

Basically, the tarot consists of two parts: the Major Arcana and the Minor Arcana. The Major Arcana is made up of 22 cards; the figures of the Major Arcana represent universal archetypes which serve as the basic patterns for human thoughts and emotions, as well as dramatic, life-changing events. For example, the Hermit can represent the need to withdraw, to seek solitude, or to look for a new direction. If you draw this card while trying to decide where your plot goes next, it could mean that your hero is about to leave everything he knows behind and embark on a solitary journey or adventure.

There are 56 cards in the Minor Arcana. While the Major Arcana expresses universal themes, the Minor Arcana brings those themes down to the practical arena and applies them to everyday life. The Minor Arcana has four suits — typically called Wands, Cups, Swords, and Pentacles — and each suit has ten numbered cards and four Court Cards (King, Queen, Knight, and Page). Each of the tarot's four suits corresponds to one of the elements: fire, earth, air, or water:

■The wands represent fire: someone with a fiery personality; tempers flaring; something is about to go up in flames; literally, something catches on fire.

■The cups represent water: someone who is very emotional; intuition; a desire or want; the beginning of a love affair.

■The swords represent air: someone who is very intellectual; using words as weapons; ideas coming into conflict; having interests in common.

■The pentacles represent earth: someone who is very wealthy; money trouble; buying or selling real estate; an opportunity to make lots of money.

As an example, the three of swords shows a heart being pierced by three swords. If you pull out this card it's time to introduce an element of betrayal or heartbreak into your story. As further illustration, the five of wands shows five men; each is holding a wand and they appear to be working against each other. This card could symbolize that there's something in the environment that's working against the protagonist, it can represent a race or competition, or it can mean that one of your characters needs to learn to get along with others.

If you want more information on how to interpret tarot cards, there are plenty of books out there which can help you, and there's are even free online courses on the tarot online.

Example: The Empress

The Empress is tarot card 3 in the Major Arcana. The card shows a beautiful woman seated on a throne covered with soft, lush pillows.

Her gown is white — representing purity — and is decorated with pomegranates; she's wearing a crown with 12 stars representing the signs of the Zodiac; in her right hand she's holding a rod which symbolizes power; and she has a shield with the symbol for Venus, the goddess of love. Her belly shows a hint of pregnancy. In the background there's a forest with trees in various stages of life, a field of ripe wheat, and a waterfall.

From the symbolism and imagery on the card, you could come up with some of the following possible meanings to apply to your story:

One of you main characters wants to become pregnant.

■An unplanned pregnancy creates a conflict in the story (maybe one character wants to keep the baby and the other doesn't).

■It can refer to motherly traits that are present in your character, or that your character meets someone new who has these traits. For example, in the Fairy Tale Tarot the Empress is represented by Cinderella's fairy godmother.

■As an outcome, this card can be a sign of prosperity (notice the abundance that surrounds the Empress).

■It's also a card of creativity; creative seeds are planted and will flourish and grow. It can represent an idea that's beginning to take shape: an idea for a new business, for a marketing campaign, and so on.
■If you pull out this card when you're trying to come up with a setting, it can represent a warm, inviting home filled with good food and laughter.

■The card can be a warning that your character needs to learn patience: just as everything in nature grows according to cycles, everything happens in due time.

■The card can also refer to a situation that is pregnant with promise.

■If the empress is surrounded by negative cards in a reading, it could signify the negative side of motherhood: over-protectiveness, smothering, and refusal to let go.

■If the card is reversed it can mean domestic upheaval, infertility, an unwanted pregnancy, or suppressed artistic expression.

■In the Wizard's Tarot—in which the Major Arcana represents the faculty at a magic school—the Empress is represented by the Professor of Herbal Magic.

A spread is a layout of the cards with a definite purpose in mind. Spreads can be simple—even one card can be a spread—or they can be very elaborate: there's one spread that uses all 78 cards. Set the intent to create a scene for your story, shuffle your cards, and pull one out at random. Write your scene based on the card that you selected.

Now set the intent to establish the setting for your story and go through the process again. You can follow this process for anything that you want to know about your story: start a dialogue, suggest a plot twist, bring a supporting character into the conflict, and so on.

Instead of one card, you can use two cards and balance them against each other: the pros and cons of a venture your protagonist is considering, a heated argument between two characters, and so on.

One way to use a three card spread is to have the cards represent your character's past, present, and future. You can also set the intent to determine the following:

■The first card represents your character's primary goal and motivation.

■The second card represents your character's greatest fear in relation to this goal.

■The third card explores the internal conflict your character has to conquer along the way.

■You can go into more detail by having larger spreads. For example, shuffle the cards and set the intent that the first six cards you choose will represent, in order, the following:

1. Protagonist: this card represents your main character.
2. Antagonist: this card represents the main adversary.
3. Theme: this card represents your novel's theme.
4. Beginning: this card represents the beginning of your novel.
5. Middle: this card represents the middle of your novel.
6. End: this card represents the end of your novel.

You can even create intricate character profiles by pulling out several cards and assigning them meanings, such as the following:

- Relationship with mother
- Relationship with father
- Relationship with siblings.
- What was the defining moment in the character's life?
- What was their first job?
- What are some of the character's idiosyncrasies or quirks?
- What's their greatest fear?
- What do they want most out of life?
- What are their major strengths?
- What are their major weaknesses?

The Celtic Cross Spread is a particularly good spread for setting out an intricate plot. In addition, you can come up with your own spreads: decide what you want to know, ask a question, and develop a custom-designed spread.

Using the tarot in your writing is simply about trusting yourself and allowing your subconscious to express itself. Pick a card and set it in front of you. What's the first image that you notice? What do you think it means? Do you get an overall impression from the image as a whole? What thoughts or feelings emerge? How can you apply it to your story? Write freely, without censoring yourself, based on the images and symbols that you see in the card and what they represent to you.

For a free online course in Tarot, visit:

http://learntarot.org/

4
The Power of Dreams

What Are Dreams?

Dreams are a succession of images, ideas, emotions and sensations occurring involuntarily in the mind during certain stages of sleep. The content and purpose of dreams are not fully understood, though they have been a topic of speculation and interest throughout recorded history.

Dreams are the gateway to the subconscious mind, and give us our only real glimpse into this vast universe of imagery. As a creative tool, dreams offer yet another way to access ideas and symbols; dreams are the lifeblood of the creative mind.

Dreams were historically used for healing (as in the asclepieions found in the ancient Greek temples of Asclepius) as well as for guidance or divine inspiration. Some Native American tribes used vision quests as a rite of passage, fasting and praying until an anticipated guiding dream was received, to be shared with the rest of the tribe upon their return.

During the late 19th and early 20th centuries, both Sigmund Freud and Carl Jung identified dreams as an interaction between the unconscious and the conscious. They also assert together that the unconscious is the dominant force of the dream, and in dreams it conveys its own mental activity to the perceptive faculty. While Freud felt that there was an active censorship against the unconscious even during sleep, Jung argued that the dream's bizarre quality is an efficient language, comparable to poetry and uniquely capable of revealing the underlying meaning.

Fritz Perls presented his theory of dreams as part of the holistic nature of Gestalt therapy. Dreams are seen as projections of parts of the self that have been ignored, rejected, or suppressed. Jung argued that one could consider every person in the dream to represent an aspect of the dreamer, which he called the subjective approach to dreams. Perls expanded this point of view to say that even inanimate objects in the dream may represent aspects of the dreamer. The dreamer may therefore be asked to imagine being an object in the dream and to describe it, in order to bring into awareness the characteristics of the object that correspond with the dreamer's personality.

There are several kinds of dreams we will concert ourselves with here, those are nightdreams and daydreams, and a component of nightdreams we call lucid dreaming.

Nightdreams occur during the REM stage of sleep, and are the most difficult to remember. The most effective way to capture their meaning and decipher their symbolism is to write them down immediately on awakening.

Dreams can contain the answer to a nagging problem, a story solution, or provide the seed of an idea that can blossom into a fully realized writing project.

Jung said that in analyzing one's own dreams that there is no delimitative guide to their meanings; each person's dreams are unique onto themselves and can only be interpreted by the person dreaming them. (Although, interestingly, studies have shown that people in general worldwide dream of the same things.)

Freud argued that all dreams contain universal symbolism; water representing sex, or birds representing freedom and so on.

To whichever school you subscribe, your dreams can provide you with rich material for creativity.

A *daydream* is a visionary fantasy, especially one of happy, pleasant thoughts, hopes or ambitions, imagined as coming to pass, and experienced while awake. There are many different types of daydreams, and there is no consistent definition amongst psychologists.

The general public also uses the term for a broad variety of experiences. Research by Harvard psychologist Deirdre Barrett has found that people who experience vivid dream-like mental images reserve the word for these, whereas many other people refer to milder imagery, realistic future planning, review of past memories or just "spacing out"--i.e. one's mind going relatively blank — when they talk about "daydreaming."

While daydreaming has long been derided as a lazy, non-productive pastime, it is now commonly acknowledged that daydreaming can be constructive in some contexts, such as in creative pursuits.

There are numerous examples of people in creative or artistic careers, such as composers, novelists and filmmakers, developing new ideas through daydreaming. Similarly, research scientists, mathematicians and physicists have developed new ideas by daydreaming about their subject areas.

Therapist Dan Jones looked at patterns in how people achieved success from entrepreneurs like

Richard Branson and Peter Jones to geniuses like Albert Einstein and Leonardo da Vinci.

Jones also looked at the thinking styles of successful creative people like Beethoven and Walt Disney. What he found was that they all had one thing in common. They all spent time daydreaming about their area of success.

So, while relaxing from your writing, feel free to let your mind drift, for daydreaming is yet another gateway to the subconscious.

Sleep and the Hypnagogic State

The strange state of mind you pass through when first falling asleep is called the hypnagogic state. First studied by Baillarger in 1846 and named by Maury in 1848, hypnagogic phenomena have been experienced by about 70% of the adult population.

Writers have long exploited their hypnagogic dreams or nightmares in order to produce extraordinary results, notably two writers of Gothic novels. Mary Shelley dreamt up the idea for Frankenstein, deemed to be the first science fiction novel, after a waking dream or nightmare during which she saw 'the pale student of unhallowed arts kneeling beside the thing he had put together'. This was to be the story of Victor Frankenstein and the repercussions of his thirst for knowledge. Bram stoker too was to be struck with the idea for his vampire novel, Dracula, whist having a nightmare. Following his nightmare he noted,

'Young man goes out, sees girls - one tries to kiss him not on the lips but throat. Old Count interferes - rage & fury diabolical - this man belongs to me I want him.' The idea he conceived in his dream became part of the journal of one of the protagonists of Dracula, Jonathan Harker: 'I suppose I must have fallen asleep; I hope so, but I fear... I cannot in the least believe that it was all sleep... ' It is clear, then, that accessing the subconscious, in hypnagogic dreams has led to the genesis of many wonderful and unique stories and poems.

Painters too have been stimulated by their dreams. The surrealists are particularly well known for this, Dali being the most famous of those.

Hypnagogic sensations that occur immediately before waking up can be extremely lucid and stimulating. One method used by Dali was to nap while sitting in an arm chair holding a spoon over a pan so that when his muscles relaxed he'd drop the spoon into the pan which would wake him up and he would have the vivid hypnagogic images fresh in his mind for him to paint.

Common hallucinations while falling asleep are faces and geometric patterns. Such hallucinations are not a sign of mental abnormality, although they can be startling if they appear unexpectedly.

Sparks of inspiration in the form of solutions of problems are another benefit of hypnagogia. Einstein's notion of relativity is said to have come to him early one morning as he got out of bed, after having researched the matter for ten years.

Thomas Edison is known to have made use of the hypnagogic state to help him formulate ideas for his inventions. The French mathematician, Hadamard, stated, ' One phenomenon is certain and I can vouch for its absolute certainty; the sudden and immediate appearance of a solution at the very moment of sudden awakening'.

I have experienced this myself; I can be frustrated at my lack of progress on a piece of work and come up with an excellent new take on things in my sleep. When I've woken up I'm able to get straight to it and sort the problem out.

According to Mavromatis, creativity can spark up unconsciously during sleep and come to the individual on waking. However, some people are able to communicate the problem that needs solving to the unconscious and the problem is solved in hypnagogia. It appears that thinking about the problem before you fall asleep, willing your unconscious to take heed, can help you to gain the solution to the problem you need.

If you aren't fortunate enough to have hypnagogic dreams, it may be possible for you to train yourself to have lucid dreams like those that sometimes accompany hypnagogia.

According to J. Allan Hobson, Professor of Psychiatry at Harvard Medical School, the techniques required to induce lucid dreaming can be acquired by anyone.

In his work *Dreaming: A Very Short Introduction* he instructs that you need to keep a notepad and pen by your bedside to record your dream.

Keeping a record when you awake is important because there are so many elements in dreams that are quickly forgotten. Hobson relates that before you go to sleep you should think that, as a human being you are likely to have two hours of 'absolutely fabulous' dreaming tonight.

You need to tune into some of it by noticing the bizarreness when it occurs. When he wants to dream lucidly he tells himself to notice things that could not happen in waking life but typically happen in dreams, such as 'the changes of the times, places and people (especially the unusual occurrence of unidentified characters, characters with the qualities of one person who suddenly have those of another, and so on)'.

Once you have done this, you should, apparently, find part of your mind waking up and you will recognize that you are dreaming and say this to yourself. The result is that part of your brain is in a waking state and the rest is in a dreaming state. Hobson states that this is where the fun begins it seems and you should be able to do whatever you wish to, such as 'fly and have whatever sorts of intimate relationships with other chosen dream characters'. Is that not an incentive to try it out?

Psychologist Thore Nielsen of Hospital du Sacre-Coeur in Montreal was interested in the hypnagogic state, so he trained himself to fall asleep at his computer. That way he could wake up when he had a hypnagogic hallucination and immediately record its content. He recorded 240 hallucinations this way.

Most of the images involved movement. The most common recurring image was "falling or stepping out into space" (Adler, 1993). This could be a measurement effect: an effect on the data caused by the nature of the measurement.

Going to sleep in front of his computer, Nielsen was in constant danger of losing muscle tone and falling to the floor, which might account for the repeated images of falling into space.

What causes hypnagogic imagery? The simplest assumption is that the hypnagogic state is an early-occurring dream fragment. This assumption is also consistent with reports that hypnagogic images are dreamlike. A subject in a 1930s experiment on hypnagogic imagery said, "These things [hypnagogic images] are practically dreams, but I am awake enough to catch them."

The adjective "hypnagogic" is a term coined by Alfred Maury for the transitional state between wakefulness and sleep (i.e. the onset of sleep). The equivalent transition to wakefulness is termed the hypnopompic state.

The term "hypnagogia" is employed by Dr Mavromatis to include both sleep onset and the transition from sleep to wakefulness; he retains, however, the adjectives "hypnagogic" and "hypnopompic" for the identification of specific experiences

Early references to hypnagogia are to be found in the writings of Aristotle, Iamblichus, Cardano, Simon Forman and Swedenborg.

Romanticism brought a renewed interest in the subjective experience of the edges of sleep. In more recent centuries, many authors have referred to the state; Edgar Allan Poe, for example, wrote of the "fancies" he experienced "only when I am on the brink of sleep, with the consciousness that I am so."

Serious scientific enquiry began in the 19th century with Johannes Peter Müller, Jules Baillarger and Alfred Maury, and continued into the twentieth with Leroy.

The advent of electroencephalography (EEG) has supplemented the introspective methods of these early researchers with physiological data. The search for neural correlates for hypnagogic imagery began with Davis et al. in the 1930s, and continues with increasing sophistication to this day.

While the dominance of the behaviorist paradigm led to a decline in research, especially in the English speaking world, the later 20th century has seen a revival, with investigations of hypnagogia and related ASCs playing an important role in the emerging multidisciplinary study of consciousness.

Much remains to be understood about the experience and its corresponding neurology, and the topic has been somewhat neglected in comparison with sleep and dreams; hypnagogia has been described as a well-trodden and yet unmapped territory.

The hypnagogic state can provide insight into a problem, the best known example being August Kekulé's realization that the structure of benzene was a closed ring after dozing in front of a fire and seeing molecules forming into snakes, one of which grabbed its tail in its mouth.

Many other artists, writers, scientists and inventors—including Beethoven, Richard Wagner, Walter Scott, Salvador Dalí, Thomas Edison and Isaac Newton—have credited hypnagogia and related states with enhancing their creativity. A 2001 study by Harvard psychologist Deirdre Barrett found that, while problems can also be solved in full-blown dreams from later stages of sleep, hypnagogia was especially likely to solve problems which benefit from hallucinatory images being critically examined while still before the eyes.

This state can be utilized to tap the creative unconscious in the development of story ideas, characters and plotlines, as well as to solve plotting and character motivational problems.

Whether you feel that you have experienced hypnagogia or not, it seems that too few people utilise their dreams or even pay any attention to them.

Dreams can stimulate, inspire and be entertaining as well. They are too often forgotten when it's clear that they could have a large influence on you in terms of creativity and summoning up original ideas and this could be a devastating waste of potential.

When we spend as much as third of our lives in sleep, is it not worth trying to get as much out of these seemingly wasted hours as we can?

Using Hypnagogia for Creativity

Many artists, writers, mystics, philosophers and scientists have used hypnagogia to break through creative brick walls. These have included Aristotle, the Greek philosopher; Robert Desnos, the French surrealist poet; Edgar Allan Poe, the American writer; Isaac Newton, the English scientist; and Beethoven, the German composer. Observed hypnagogia can inspire not just images and sounds, but also present flashes of insight and, occasionally, genius.

Hypnagogic states are highly creative. They are extremely productive, packing a high density of ideas into a short period of time. They are extremely novel, throwing together ideas and thoughts that might never have occured to you otherwise. They express the incredible flexibility of the mind. They are more complex than you can grasp in a wakeful state. They transform existing objects into something totally new.

But the best part is that we all have access to this state. We can do it as much as we like without doing harm to ourselves and it will become more productive the more we use it. Think again of Thomas Edison. Was he a particularly innovative inventor? Or was he just some guy who napped a lot? The two go hand in hand. Walk hand in hand with your unconscious, work together.

As you develop your ability to enter a hypnagogic state, you can start to try and do more with these experiences. You can't directly control the hallucinations, but you can try to suggest things to the mind. It is important that you remain relaxed. Just let it happen, whatever it is. Anxiety will provoke your alarm systems and you will wake up. The hallucination is in control just as much as you.

Of course, the hypnagogic experience is just an entertainment unless you make an attempt to record it. If you want to make something creative out of the hallucination then you must rehearse and write it down immediately afterwards, while you are still in the afterglow of the experience, otherwise it will fade quickly and vanish.

Another way to record the experience is to learn to verbally report the images as they are happening using a dictaphone. This is not easy to do in the beginning because it uses the analytical side of the brain, which is inherently wakeful, but it can be done. Verbal reporting can take place as long as you don't search for words, grammar or intellectual concern for the expression of abstract ideas. This means that you can record more directly the images and ideas, rather than scrabbling for a pen immediately afterwards.

Inspiration gained from hypnagogic states can also be used to ease creative pressure on an artist and to deflate ego and arrogance. Because they are ideas that have arrived from an unconscious state, it is hard to take full credit for them. The creative process becomes more of a partnership between you and your 'muse'. Tom Waits is among the many artists who have found this a useful way of reducing the stress of public acclamation of his 'talent'. He puts in his shift and his muse puts in hers. When the ideas arrive, he is ready to receive and works them up into songs or words. If the ideas don't arrive, then it's not his fault; he did his job and his muse simply failed to show up, maybe she will tomorrow.

Reaching the Hypnagogic State

STEP ONE

The most crucial part of experiencing this profound state of mind is simply to learn how to relax, or let go. This can be achieved by performing a progressive relaxation technique, which is when you gradually focus on tensing and relaxing all the parts of the body, from your toes to your head. Continue your practices throughout the day whenever you have spare time, and see how your ability let go improves over time. Hypnagogia can only occur when you are deeply soothed, so you must learn to lose control so your body can show its more subtle side. This will hopefully facilitate the access to the creative mind.

STEP TWO

Once you acquire the necessary aptitude for relaxing, the next step is to organize a proper time to practice your technique. The most effective method is to set your alarm to the early morning hours, staying up for at least thirty minutes to allow yourself to regain awareness. Engage in some sort of stimulating activity while building up your intention to observe the unconscious mind. If possible, generate a mantra that you will actively repeat to remind yourself of the important task at hand. Some people like to take caffeine before their attempt to improve their success rate even more, but this is not completely necessary. Another ideal time is during an afternoon nap, when the human brain is at its highest level of alertness with an increase in beta waves.

STEP THREE

Slowly begin to wind down, releasing all negative thoughts and worries. After reaching a state of reasonable serenity, there may be an increase in strange or intrusive thoughts that may distract you from your intention. The only way to prevent these abstract thoughts is by focusing on something to stay alert, thus bringing your consciousness into the sleep state. There are numerous ways to do this, but the most simple technique is to focus on your breath moving into and out of your body. While doing this, repeat your mantra in co-ordination to the breaths. In other words mentally recite 'One, I will stay alert. Two, I will stay alert' and continue to count your breaths while attentively focusing on your intention. Some people prefer to use visualization to induce the mysterious state faster, which involves engaging all of your senses in the scene. For instance, some people imagine climbing up stairs or driving a car, while really trying to experience it as if it's actually happening. This will also keep you aware and bring you closer to conscious sleep.

STEP FOUR

Watch for any signs of bright colors or patterns emerging in front of your eyes. Do not try to control these shapes, just observe quietly and keep your mind on your intention to stay aware. Keep in mind that the imagery is hypnotic and can rapidly cause you to lose awareness. Watch it indirectly to prevent this from happening. Eventually, as the state deepens you will begin to hear voices or see scenes. Hypnagogia can include all of your five senses, even your sense of taste and smell. Sometimes, music or poetry will be heard, but the context in this state often uses various forms of wordplay. Scenes will often blend into each other or simply float around, and can be either extremely lifelike or rather vague. Just enjoy the ride, and when you wake up, immediately record any prior experiences. This will help you develop new creative insight or ideas.

- Hypnagogia is about observing the mind as it descends into Stage 1 sleep. Therefore, the two prerequisites are drowsiness AND an effort to think. Just drowsiness and you risk falling asleep; just an effort to think and your mind will stay awake. It is the effort to think that makes it possible to 'observe' the consciousness of your subconscious mind.

- Therefore, don't try it when you are tired. Late night hypnagogia will probably just lead to full-on sleep.
- If you think that sleep is a risk, don't use your bed. If you do use your bed, perhaps prop yourself up with a pillow to avoid sleep.
- Follow Thomas Edison's guide. Get yourself some steel balls and an armchair. Another one I've heard is a teaspoon and a plate. Hold the teaspoon in your hand and put the plate on the floor underneath. You'll wake when you muscles relax and the teaspoon drops onto the plate.
- Try setting your alarm for 30 minutes earlier in the morning and then try to 'doze', try to balance between sleep and wakefulness until it is time for you to get up.
- You can use the snooze alarm on your clock to make sure you don't go into sleep.
- The afternoon nap is another classic opportunity for hypnagogia.
- The brain works in roughly 90 minute high activity cycles, each followed by a 20 minute low activity cycle. If you can, work for 90 minutes and then try a burst of hypnagogia.
- Stage 1 of sleep only lasts about five minutes. If you wake up after twenty, you've probably been asleep.
- Relax, close your eyes, but stay watchful, observe yourself drifting off.

- Try concentrating on the changing patterns of your mind as you drop off. Don't think about what you are thinking about (i.e. work, the kids, etc.), but just observe the way in which your thinking is changing, a change in consciousness perhaps.
- For me, there's a point where I feel the body go numb (sleep paralysis) and then I know that in a few seconds my mind will dip into subconscious activity. If I don't fall asleep, I know that I will be able to observe this state.
- Be patient. At first this will seem like an odd thing to be doing and you will probably struggle to enter a hypnagogic state. Keep trying, but don't force it.

Lucid Dreaming

A lucid dream, in simplest terms, is a dream in which one is aware that one is dreaming. The term was coined by the Dutch psychiatrist and writer Frederik van Eeden (1860–1932).

A lucid dream can begin in one of two ways. A dream-initiated lucid dream (DILD) starts as a normal dream, and the dreamer eventually concludes it is a dream, while a wake-initiated lucid dream (WILD) occurs when the dreamer goes from a normal waking state directly into a dream state, with no apparent lapse in consciousness.

Lucid dreaming has been researched scientifically, and its existence is well established.

Scientists such as Stephen LaBerge and Allan Hobson, with his neurophysiological approach to dream research, have helped to push the understanding of lucid dreaming into a less speculative realm.

The ability to become aware during the dream that one is dreaming takes practice. The benefit is that by becoming aware, you will be able to directly access the subconscious mind and in some cases be able to guide the dream while you are having it.

One technique for doing this is called Wake Initiated Lucid Dreaming. (WILD)

The wake-initiated lucid dream occurs when "the sleeper enters REM sleep with unbroken self-awareness directly from the waking state".

There are many techniques aimed at entering a WILD. The key to these techniques is recognizing the hypnagogic stage, which is within the border of being awake and being asleep. If a person is successful in staying aware while this stage occurs, that person will eventually enter the dream state while being fully aware that it is a dream.

There are key times when this state is best entered. While success at normal bedtime after having been awake all day is difficult, it is relatively easy after sleeping for 3–7 hours or in the afternoon during a nap.

Techniques for inducing WILDs abound. Dreamers may count, envision themselves climbing or descending stairs, chant to themselves, control their breathing, count their breaths to keep their thoughts from drifting.

They may also concentrate on relaxing their body from their toes to their head, or allow images to flow through their "mind's eye" and envision themselves jumping into the image to maintain concentration and keep their mind awake, while still being calm enough to let their bodies sleep.

During the actual transition into the dream state, dreamers are likely to experience sleep paralysis, including rapid vibrations, a sequence of loud sounds, and a feeling of twirling into another state of body awarenes, or of "drifting off into another dimension", or like passing the interface between water into air, face front, body first, or the gradual sharpening and becoming "real" of images or scenes they are thinking of and trying to visualize gradually, which they can actually "see", instead of the indefinite sensations they feel when trying to imagine something while wide awake.

Dreams and Nightmares

Dreams are the pathways to our inner souls and come from our subconscious mind. While we are sleeping, our body tries to send messages about the wants and needs our body. A person's dreams can give a sense of direction in life. Even though we cannot remember, a majority of our dreams when we wake up still have an impact on the way we think and function. Sigmund Freud believed that dreams are expressions of unfulfilled wishes and desires.

Dreaming plays an important role in our lives. Studies have shown that people who are repeatedly awakened at the beginning of dream periods for several nights become irritable and have difficulty concentrating. If your bodies' natural sleep cycle has been interrupted and has been deprived of dream sleep, your body will compensate by providing proportionately more dream sleep at the next dream sleep opportunity. Research shows that a healthy sleep is needed for a person's body to restore itself. Some scientists believe that adequate dream sleep is equally important because it enables the brain to recharge.

Medical research has not proven this testimony. Usually, when a person is awake, their brain waves will show a regular rhythm. When a person first falls asleep, the brain waves become slower and less regular. They call this sleep state non-rapid eye movement (NREM) sleep.

NREM sleep consists of stages. There are four stages and each stage is a progressively deeper stage. The deeper the sleep, the more your body restores itself. Stage one sleep is the transition from wakefulness to sleep. Restoration begins in stage two, but is more significant in stages three and four, sometimes called delta sleep.

After an hour and a half of NREM sleep, the brain waves begin to show a more active pattern again, though the individual is in a deep sleep. These sleep states are called rapid eye movement (REM) sleep, is when dreaming occurs. A person typically experiences a brief arousal from sleep and returns to stage two sleep after dreaming. This sleep cycle has begun again. The length of time in each of these stages differs throughout the night, with most REM sleep occurring during the later sleep cycle.

Writing Down The Dream

"I had the most amazing dream, it was right there until I woke up and then it evaporated!" Our nightly dreams can be fleeting. They can also offer such helpful and important guidance that they are well worth trying to retain. There is a way to train your brain to hold onto dream material and it's not hard to do, nor is it expensive.

The magic key is to write your dreams down. Keeping a dream journal is a hugely satisfying endeavor and the very act of making them important enough to record helps the unconscious mind realize their value, thus pulling them out of sleep more often.

Asking yourself a few extra questions will make your dreamwork even more useful. Note anything unusual about your day. We often dream about the day we've just lived, but it can be hard to remember weeks later when you took your pet to the vet, or paid that parking ticket. Writing it down with the date will make it easier to determine if your dream is related to your activities.

The subconscious mind uses our dreams to mull over conflicts and concerns. Perhaps the lack of conscious-state distractions makes this time especially advantageous. Nearly everyone has had the experience of waking with an answer to a question they went to bed pondering.

Additional sources may influence our dreams as well. Many indigenous cultures hold the tenant that our souls or spirits can leave the confines of our physical bodies during sleep and that they can visit with the spirits of ancestors and the living as well.

Numerous people report having dreams of departed loved ones, including messages shared in these visitation dreams. Others, including a great many in the Holy Bible, have been given messages by angels in their dreams.

Innovations in science, the arts, sports, medicine and spiritual evolution have all come from dreams. The Periodic Table of elements was organized in a dream.

Billy Joel and Paul McCartney, among many other composers, dream lyrics and melodies. The test to prove that insulin was effective in the treatment of diabetes came in a dream. Many people have dreams that dictate personal diagnosis and healing suggestions. Additionally, most religions have pivotal dreams in the forming of their sacred structures.

Intuition and spiritual inspiration have come to countless people in their nightly nocturnal dramas. So I invite you to begin writing yours down. Ask yourself how you felt when you woke and jot that down as well. For me, remembering, journaling and working with my dreams is like taping into our spiritual source. My dreams restore me, they inspire me and they offer welcome guidance.

If in a state of consciousness that lies between reality and the world of dreams. The imagination roams freely, although usually guided by unconscious urges, concerns and memories.

During this time of dreaming and fantasizing, you can focus on anything you want, including making goals for yourself on how you are going to live your whole life.

Dreams can stay in your mind, no one has to know about them, and you can record them, in a dream journal, where you write down your significant dreams and fantasies. These dreams and fantasies can be used as motivators to help you work on your inner motivations, demons and desires.

H.P. Lovecraft claimed in a letter to his friend Frank Long that he never actively tried to write a story, but instead waited until he was gripped by the feeling that it had to be written.

Lovecraft was possessed by an astonishingly vivid dream life. This was central to his life as a writer, since he drew many of the characters, settings, place names, and entire plots of his stories directly from these nocturnal visions.

He wrote his apocalyptic prose poem "Nyarlathotep," for example, after a fantastically vivid and horrifying nightmare in which not only the title word but the entire story was given to him virtually intact. The piece in its finished form is essentially a dream transcript, and its powerful oneiric quality is surely due to the fact that he leapt out of bed and wrote most of it before he was fully awake.

"The Statement of Randolph Carter," describing a nocturnal descent into a tomb, had a similar origin. The bat-winged "Night Gaunts" of his dreamland stories came directly from his boyhood nightmares.

In commenting on the fact that these "compelling impulses" were communicated directly to Lovecraft by his dreams, the French literary scholar Maurice Lévy makes an interesting observation about its import for Lovecraft's creativity:

"When he tried to write by forcing himself, the result was flat and cold. He knew not how to compose a worthwhile tale except under the incitement of dream. He even carried this scruple to the point of wondering whether those works he wrote in this other state ought truly to be considered his own" (Lovecraft: A Study in the Fantastic, 1988).

The Dream Journal

A dream journal (or dream diary) is a journal in which dream experiences are recorded. A dream journal might include a record of nightly dreams, personal reflections and waking dream experiences. It is often used in the study of dreams and psychology.

Dream journals are also used by people trying to lucid dream.

They are also regarded as a useful catalyst for remembering dreams. The use of a dream diary was recommended by Ann Faraday in The Dream Game as an aid to memory and a way to preserve details, many of which are otherwise rapidly forgotten no matter how memorable the dream originally seemed.

The very act of recording a dream can have the effect of improving future dream recall. Keeping a dream journal conditions a person to view remembering dreams as important. Traditionally, dreams have been recorded in a paper journal (as text, drawings, paintings, etc.) or via an audio recording device (as narrative, music or imitations

of other auditory experiences from the dream.)
Now with the internet, many sites offer the ability
to create a digital dream journal.

The dream journal can be a wonderful resource for
story ideas, since it is a reflection of thoughts and
ideas culled from the subconscious mind and put
down to paper.

The description of the dream can contain symbols
and ideas that when used as a springboard for
stimulating creativity, can result in full blown
stories, characters and plotlines.

How to Create A Dream Journal

1. Select a notebook specifically to record your
dreams in. A nice fancy journal or a blank
bounded book may encourage you to use it.

However, a plain spiral notebook or paper
pad will also suffice. Keep it by your bedside
where it is easily accessible. Dream details fade
quickly after awakening so it is essential to record
the dream immediately.

2. Keep a consistent dream format. Date each
dream entry. It doesn't matter if you use last
night's date or the next morning as long you keep
it consistent.

3. Write in the PRESENT tense as if the dream is
still occurring before your eyes. This helps to

recall your dreams by putting you back into the moment of your dream.

4. Write down every possible detail of you dream. Location, colors, sounds, objects, characters, and your emotions are all important aspects of your dream. You may want to ask yourself the following questions.

- What are the significant images or symbols in your dream?

- Where is the dream located? What is in the scene or what is the landscape like? What is the ambience or mood of the dream?

- Who else is in the dream?

- How does the dream make you feel? What is your mood when you first wake up from the dream?

- How does your dream parallel a situation or experience in your waking life?

5. Grammar, spelling and punctuation are not important when recording your dreams. Just get the dream down on paper before it slips away and record everything that you remember even if it may only be fragments.

As you start writing, more and more pieces of the dreams will come to you. Because we are not able to write faster than what we are thinking, it may be a good idea to record your dreams on tape first.

It will still be a good idea to go back and document the dream on paper.

6. When something is hard to describe in words, draw a quick sketch of the imagery. Color pencils or crayons may help depict your picture more clearly.

7. After you have record your dream, make a little footnote of any major concerns or issues that is going on in your waking life. As your journal grows, you may see a correlation and pattern between your dream and reality.

8. Put a title on it, if you'd like.

9. Highlight keywords, symbols, characters or themes that stand out. It may be helpful to keep an appendix or a glossary of personal dream themes. You will start to develop a pattern and formulate your own significance to these dream themes.

5

Creative Blocks

What Are Creative Blocks?

Creative blocks, more commonly known as 'Writer's Block', is a condition, associated with writing as a profession, in which an author loses the ability to produce new work. The condition varies widely in intensity. It can be trivial, a temporary difficulty in dealing with the task at hand. At the other extreme, some "blocked" writers have been unable to work for years on end, and some have even abandoned their careers. It can manifest as the affected writer viewing their work as inferior or unsuitable, when in fact it could be the opposite.

Causes of Writer's Block

Writer's block may have many or several causes. Some are essentially creative problems that originate within an author's work itself. A writer may run out of inspiration. The writer may be greatly distracted and feel he or she may have something that needs to be done beforehand.

A project may be fundamentally misconceived, or beyond the author's experience or ability. A fictional example can be found in George Orwell's novel Keep The Aspidistra Flying, in which the protagonist Gordon Comstock struggles in vain to complete an epic poem describing a day in London:

"It was too big for him, that was the truth. It had never really progressed, it had simply fallen apart into a series of fragments."

Other blocks, especially the more serious kind, may be produced by adverse circumstances in a writer's life or career: physical illness, depression, the end of a relationship, financial pressures, a sense of failure.

The pressure to produce work may in itself contribute to a writer's block, especially if they are compelled to work in ways that are against their natural inclination, i.e. too fast or in some unsuitable style or genre.

In some cases, writer's block may also come from feeling intimidated by a previous big success, the creator putting on themselves a paralyzing pressure to find something to equate that same success again. The writer Elizabeth Gilbert, reflecting on her post-bestseller prospects, proposes that such a pressure might be released by interpreting creative writers as "having" genius rather than "being" a genius.

In George Gissing's New Grub Street, one of the first novels to take writer's block as a main theme, the novelist Edwin Reardon becomes completely unable to write and is shown as suffering from all those problems.

In her 2004 book The Midnight Disease: The Drive to Write, Writer's Block, and the Creative Brain (ISBN 9780618230655), the writer and neurologist Alice W. Flaherty has argued that literary creativity is a function of specific areas of the brain, and that block may be the result of brain activity being disrupted in those areas.

How to Overcome Them

Often the "block" is really procrastination disguised as a "block." If one is being diligent and honest with oneself, by sitting at your workspace each day at the allotted time, and working through the lack of motivation to write will eventually bring about positive results.

There are times when the ideas simply won't come; when the answer to a particular plot line or character problem or book outline just won't become apparent to us.

This is a good of time as any to use some tricks and tools to "breakout" of the logjam. Free Association, Free Writing, Tarot Cards, even daydreaming can get your creative juices flowing again.

If you find that day after day has gone by and nothing is happening, you may wish to put down that particular project for awhile and work on something fresh.

Often by working on two or three different projects concurrently can get your mind to not dwell too long on one particular set of ideas and this can in and of itself provide the solution.

The most common type of "writers block" I've seen is where a writer is simply waiting for inspiration to strike to begin writing. So the writer watches TV, lounges on the couch, takes naps, plays video games, talks on the phone or cruises the internet until the grand flash hits.

Except it never does.

So as each day passes, the writer's anxiety grows and the more he thinks he's blocked, the more blocked he becomes until he can't bring himself to even think about writing, let alone sit down and try to do it.

This isn't really a writers block.

It's sloth, plain and simple.

It is the writer succumbing to the procrastinating, lazy mind that is trying to avoid the anxiety of writing and in the process ends up creating an even larger problem: the anxiety of being blocked!

And it's surprisingly easy to fall into the trap of laziness and believe it's a block.

It's nonsense if you believe it's a block, and you will need to be disciplined enough to stay the course and not let the squirrely mind run shotgun over your progress if you are to move forward in your creative endeavors.

Even if you do not feel like writing or think you are blocked, you must shut up and show up at your workspace, even if you just sit there and stare into space.

If you are putting in the time, if you are "suiting up and showing up" as it were, and day after the day the muse does not show up, then I would advise you use some of the tools in the later chapter to help get those creative juices flowing again.

Author Julia Cameron advocates the practice of morning pages as a remedy to writer's block. Morning pages are 3 handwritten pages of free writing where the purpose is to write without the intention of using the writing for anything. It is a practice that can bring your thoughts to the surface and allow you enter a more creative zone.

Very often "writer's block" is not a block at all and the faster you move past this stage the better off you'll be and the sooner you'll be happily creating again.

If you continue to be blocked over an extended period, you may be having inner conflicts about your life, your motivation and your purpose.

In cases like this, a complete change or break may be in order.

'Creative blocks' come from people's life journeys. If you don't know who you are or what you're about or what you believe in it's really pretty impossible to be creative. So I think a lot of times when people have "creative blocks" and I know my share of friends do as well if they're at just some stuck point. They're not sure what to do with their lives or their writing or their photography or their filmmaking or whatever it is that they're doing. I think the best advice is you have to change your life up completely; to go on a trip, to go spend a year being of service. Be

willing to take some major drastic action to get you out of your comfort zone and go inside, not outside."

~ *Rainn Wilson*

Eliminating Doubt - Suspending Judgment

Although doubt is a natural part of the creative process, the trick is to accept it and then put it aside. There are two sides to writing, the first is writing without judgment, the second is to rewrite with a more objective editorial view.

True creativity from the subconscious contains no judgments, no inner critic, and no self-doubt, much like the flower has no doubt as it grows.

Second guessing, judging, inner conflict and self-criticism will serve only to stop the flow of ideas and shut down your progress. Give yourself the freedom to create without doubt.

Suspend judgment and allow the muse to guide you. Many artists do this all the time - they call it 'throwing paint on the canvas.' They simply let the "spirit" guide them as they hurl colors and blobs of paint onto the blank slate of canvas, watching the interplay of random colors and in that interplay and experimentation new forms emerge that can in and of themselves inspire and spark new creative ideas.

"If you're sitting out there now with a talent in your chest I promise you that talent was not put out there for you to suffer. That talent was put out there for you to develop and use"

"That absolute passion of belief that says 'what I was gonna do, I'm gonna set out to do, and everything's gonna work for me. It's just that absolute sense of entitlement; it's the only way I can describe it." - *Paul Williams, Composer*

Don't Rewrite or Edit As You Go

Some writers like to write, then immediately go over what they've written and then edit or rewrite it on the spot. This is not a good idea for several reasons, but there are no etched in stone rules. We all have different work habits that work best for each of us.

Since writing is a circular process, you don't do everything in some specific order. Sometimes you write something and then tinker with it before moving on.

But be warned: there are two potential problems with revising as you go. One is that if you revise only as you go along, you never get to think of the big picture. The key is still to give yourself enough time to look at the work as a whole once you've finished.

Another danger to revising as you go is that you may short-circuit your creativity. If you spend too much time tinkering with what is on the page, you may lose some of what hasn't yet made it to the page. Here's a tip: Don't proofread as you go. You may waste time correcting the commas in a sentence that may end up being cut anyway.

Being Present When The Muse Strikes

I know we're beating a dead horse here, but I can't stress enough the importance of showing up for your creative sessions each day with a sense of purpose.

The creative muse can strike anywhere at any time, but the best way to become a productive writer and to get better at your craft is to go to your workspace each day and work at it.

If you are present when the muse strikes, that is, being in your chair in front of your computer (with the browser and internet turned off) working on your writing, you will not only coax the muse forward up from the depths of your subconscious, but you will be in the best place you can be to capture that 'lightning in a bottle' by being able to put it down on paper.

Some writers don't work at their best at a word processor. Some actually carry a portable voice recorder and dictate their writing into the recorder and transcribe it later. Some write longhand on yellow legal tablets.

This can be done in any location, I suppose, but to me any place other than a quiet distraction-free room is an invitation to scare away the muse.

Think of it this way: Let's say you have a job building a house. If you show up every single day to work, but the person who hired you hasn't delivered the materials to build the house, then the house won't be built.

If, on the other hand, the materials are delivered but you're not there to receive them, the guy who delivered the materials might just decide that you don't need them, and he'll take them away again.

And the house still won't be built.

It's your creative entity's job to deliver the materials.

It's your job to be there when they arrive, so you can take those materials and build something wonderful with them. That's why it's so essential to sit down and write every day, preferably at the same time. Your genius knows exactly where to find you so he can deliver the goods.

And if he doesn't show up with the delivery?

At least you were there.

The Human Dilemma of Creation

I call this the "What's the Use?" Syndrome.

Sometimes I get stuck creatively and I have absolutely no motivation.

If I explore this feeling a bit deeper, I'm struck with this sense of insignificance, that the act of writing is and of itself an exercise in futility.

The existentialist philosophers saw life this way, in their search for the meaning, and in trying to discover a sense of purpose, they came away with the rather depressing view that life is a chance flash in a cold and uncaring universe, and that death is inevitable anyway, so there is no true meaning. it just is what it is.

So why bother?

Well, if all the great artists and writers had let this feeling of hopelessness prevent them from creating, then we would not have the treasure trove of art and literature we have today.

Psychologists have studied the human dilemma of creation, and have speculated that the self-doubt possibly stems from the view that when confronted with the act of creating something (creating order from chaos) we actually have to confront facing our own mortality.

The act of writing is a preservation of a suspended moment in time, whether that moment is fictional or not, in the present tense or set in some future or past tense.

It's eternal, it's a record that we were here, and when we have gone to our graves that record will (presumably, if preserved somehow) go on to immortalize us.

In our own way, the act of creation is for each of us, our bid for immortality, our fossil in the cube.

In an interview on existential psychology, Rollo May addressed this very subject:

"We are conscious of our own selves, our own tasks, and also we know we're going to die. Man is the only creature -- men, women, and children sometimes even, are the only creatures who can be aware of their death, and out of that comes normal anxiety."

"When I let myself feel that, then I apply myself to new ideas, I write books, I communicate with my fellows. In other words, the creative interchange of human personality rests upon the fact that we know we're going to die. Of that the animals and the grass and so on know nothing. But our knowledge of our death is what gives us a normal anxiety that says to us, 'Make the most of these years you are alive.' And that's what I've tried to do."

"Being a writer means to write whether there is any reward or not. That is why a writer finds it so difficult to overcome the feeling of annoyance at any interference with his writing whether from a friend, from an editor, or even a person whom he loves above all else....

Write for the pleasure of writing only, and never think of whether of what you write is "good" or "bad." Do you wonder whether the echo of your footsteps is good or bad, whether the blink of your eye is good or bad? Writing is a bodily function for a writer and it is what it is.

It may be wise to give up the illusion of being a famous writer, a renowned writer–but it is never an illusion to think of being just a writer."

- Janet and Isaac Asimov on 'HOW TO ENJOY WRITING'

The Ivory Tower Exposed

Many writers over the years have come to believe that true effective writing can only come from being sequestered in a proverbial "ivory tower," that there is only one real location for creativity. But as was explored earlier, not all effective writing needs to be done in a quiet and pristine environment, secluded from people.

In fact, writers must engage with the world in order to be able to reflect it. Too often writers, particularly ones who consider themselves to be scholarly, become separated from the realities of everyday life,

One cannot write in a complete vacuum, at the very least, one cannot live in complete isolation from one's fellow man and expect to connect with their hopes, fears, lives and loves.

Harlan Ellison, the great fantasy writer, was so incensed about the ivory tower myth that he devised a publicity stunt with a bookstore in New York City.

He set up a table, chair and his typewriter in a storefront window and proceeded to sit in the chair for days on end and write a novel while curious passersby gawked.

At the end of it, he concluded the quality of the writing had not suffered one iota as a result of leaving the ivory tower.

This is not to say you should avoid writing in a private workspace free of distraction. We are all unique and each of us develops are own most effective environments to write in. But rest assured writing can be done anywhere: in a café, in the back of a taxi cab, in a motel room or in central park.

Double Edge Sword of Distraction

Distractions are everywhere for writers. Ringing phones, a fast DSL connection just a click away from our writing. Crying children. Barking dogs. A spouse that needs help with bringing in the groceries.

Distraction can be a good thing. Sometimes we work so hard and so long on a story or an idea that a break is helpful to recharge our batteries, get our minds off the hard focus of the work, and to allow the subconscious to work its magic.

But for me, as a writer, I need a space where I can work that is as distraction free as possible.

One's living situation really dictates the distraction level, and is not always possible, depending on your paycheck, to add on that extra soundproof room or to have a large enough home to dedicate a portion of the basement or attic to your writing area.

For a professional writer, one who needs to output a number of pages per day to stay in business, this workspace free of distraction is essential to financial survival.

For part-time or hobbyist writers, or for those who simply want to create for the sake of creating, a quiet room is a luxury, not a necessity.

Distractions come in all shapes and sizes from a paper cut to a teenager who needs to talk right now. Learn when to allow distractions and when to close the door.

Distractions are a fact of life. Learning how to effectively channel the countless interruptions and distractions into something positive is a critical skill for a writer to master. Writers come from every walk of life and work in various ways to get their jobs done. There are some significant boundaries that all writers need to have in place whether they work in Capetown or Cape Cod, in a high rise office or a back bedroom.

Prerequisite to Writing

Being unfocused isn't a bad thing as long as it is controllable. It is usually a prerequisite to writing, a period of time in which the mind floats, searching for a place to land.

That unfocused, intentional drift is an incredibly important time in which to gather ideas and choose a topic or a poem's direction.

Thornton Wilder (1897 - 1975, author of Our Town) touches on this sensory ride in his quote, "The stuff of which masterpieces are made drifts about the world waiting to be clothed in words."

Finding Your Focus

Clarity is that place where all writers suddenly feel as though a veil has been lifted and pure intention is harnessed. This is where ideas are lined up like horses at the track, ready to blaze straight out of the gates.

Once focus takes hold, the writing journey begins in earnest. George Lucas said it so succinctly, "Your focus determines your reality."

Writing Distractions

Most writers suffer from the same group of everyday, common distractions:

• phones ringing
• email overload
• home and yard work
• pets and child care
• exercise for health
• time for friends and family

If writing is what you love to do, what is the problem? Most likely, the problem comes from not setting boundaries for yourself.

Getting Organized and Setting Boundaries

When setting boundaries this includes where and when to write. Writing from a central room in a house with pets and children running around is asking for trouble. Turning off a phone does not make you a bad person.

Simple steps to create order :

- set up a writing space where interruptions will be minimal
- turn off the phone (let voice mail take over)
- allow yourself a set amount of time to read emails, check the news
- make lunch time a special time for eating, talking, being playful
- allow yourself a 30 minute time to exercise every day (walk, do Iron yoga, Pilates or Zumba)

Once you take yourself seriously as a writer, so will everyone else.

Creating order is simply creating a space in each day for writing to come first. Elizabeth Barrett Browning once said, "At painful times, when composition is impossible and reading is not enough, grammars and dictionaries are excellent for distraction." Now there's a way to regain focus!

Inspiration for Writing

Viewing distractions as inspiration in some way can help alleviate the feelings of annoyance and impatience. Stephen King said it best when he wrote, "In truth, I've found that any day's routine interruptions and distractions don't much hurt a work in progress and may actually help it in some ways. It is, after all, the dab of grit that seeps into an oyster's shell that makes the pearl."

Physiological Components

Physiological components are often overlooked when considering how our states of conscious awareness are affected and prevented from accessing the subconscious.

Writing is a sedentary occupation for most of us, and it's difficult unless one is disciplined to get regular exercise and eat properly to maintain our health at peak efficiency.

We are at our best mentally when we have taken care of ourselves physically, something quite easy to forget when we are immersed in creative activity.

Therefore, getting the right amount of rest, sleep and exercise is every bit as important for accessing our subconscious states and writing well as the act of writing itself.

Diet plays an important role here, as well.

Eating more fresh fruits and vegetables, limiting our caloric intake, keeping the white flour, sugar and salt a minimum; all these go a long way toward keeping our minds operating at a high level of functioning.

Depression is another malady that can shut a writer down, or at the least, severely limit his capacity to create.

Depression can be caused by a number of factors, some genetic. Depression can also be brought on by poor diet, lack of rest, and lack of exercise.

(For a wonderful book on diet, exercise and common sense exercise, I recommend *"Living Thin In A Fast Food World"* by Jill-Bennett, MD.)

Personally, I suffered from depression for most of my adult life until I sought help for it.

After a lot of research and diagnosis, it was found that I had genetically inherited depression, that is, that the natural level of serotonin in the brain was being passed through the cells too quickly.

It was determined by my doctors that a serotonin uptake inhibitor, such as Prozac, would help maintain the right balance. Once I found there would be no side effects in taking it, I did so and my life changed dramatically.

It has made a world of difference in my sense of well-being and functioning and my writing as a result.

In today's world, people do not have to suffer with depression any longer. If you are continually depressed, seek the help of a physician and he may recommend a regimen that will get you back on the road to recovery and living a happy, healthy life.

Depression can prevent you from becoming the great writer that sleeps within!

6

Flexing Your Creative Muscles: Exercises and Tools

Jumping Off

When you are stuck, there's nothing like jumping off the dock and right into the cold water. The longer you stand around on the dock agonizing over how cold the water is going to be, you might as well be in the water and warming up to the plunge.

First of all, starting in will empower you and propel you to move forward. There's nothing quite like "just doing something" to shake the chains of procrastination.
Free writing is a great tool to start with for getting those creative juices flowing.

The Free Writing Technique

Free writing, as we covered briefly earlier, is also called writing free stream-of-consciousness writing — is a prewriting technique in which a person writes continuously for a set period of time without regard to spelling, grammar, or topic.

It produces raw, often unusable material, but helps writers overcome blocks of apathy and self-criticism. It is used mainly by prose writers and writing teachers. Some writers use the technique to collect initial thoughts and ideas on a topic, often as a preliminary to formal writing.

Free writing is not the same as automatic writing.

Peter Elbow advanced freewriting in his book Writing Without Teachers (1975), and it has been popularized by Julia Cameron through her book The Artist's Way (1992).

Natalie Goldberg combined the notion of freewriting with Zen Buddhist meditation principles to develop writing practice, described in books such as Writing Down the Bones (1986).

Writing practice is different from freewriting encouraged in undergraduate and creative writing programs. Writing practice encourages the writer to be aware of their thoughts throughout the writing practice, and may be an end unto itself, rather than a means to produce a more polished piece.

The technique involves continuous writing, usually for a predetermined period of time (often five, ten, or fifteen minutes). The writer writes without regard to spelling, grammar, etc., and makes no corrections.

If the writer reaches a point where they can't think of anything to write, they write that they can't think of anything, until they find another line of thought. The writer freely strays off topic, letting thoughts lead where they may. At times, a writer may also do a focused freewrite, letting a chosen topic structure their thoughts. Expanding from this topic, the thoughts may stray to make connections and create more abstract views on the topic. This technique helps a writer explore a particular subject before putting ideas into a more basic context.

Freewriting is often done on a daily basis as a part of the writer's daily routine. Also, students in many writing courses are assigned to do such daily writing exercises.

Here are the essential rules that are often formulated for the beginners or students, often a paraphrase of Natalie Goldberg's "Rules for Free Writing," often referred as Natalie Goldberg's first four rules of writing:

- Give yourself a time limit. Write for one or ten or twenty minutes, and then stop.
- Keep your hand moving until the time is up. Do not pause to stare into space or to read what you've written. Write quickly but not in a hurry.
- Pay no attention to grammar, spelling, punctuation, neatness, or style. Nobody else needs to read what you produce here. The correctness and quality of what you write do not matter; the act of writing does.
- If you get off the topic or run out of ideas, keep writing anyway. If necessary, write nonsense or whatever comes into your head, or simply scribble: anything to keep the hand moving.
- If you feel bored or uncomfortable as you're writing, ask yourself what's bothering you and write about that.
- When the time is up, look over what you've written, and mark passages that contain ideas or phrases that might be worth keeping or elaborating on in a subsequent free-writing session.

Mind Maps

A "mind map" is a diagram technique commonly used to break blocks affecting creative flow. This is an affliction, known as "writer's block". Although it's suffered most notoriously by writers, it can happen in any other creative discipline.

Although the term "mind map" was coined by popular psychology author Tony Buzan, this technique has been around for centuries. Diagramming is especially useful for writers who are primarily visual thinkers.

This technique is called a mind map because it mimics the spontaneous workings of the human mind during the creative process.

On first glimpse, a typical mind map might look like a group of Daddy Longlegs spiders in a gang fight.

A mind map uses bubbles, boxes, lines, and arrows. Inside the bubbles and boxes are notations of various types, all related to the creative logjam that a writer (or other creative type) might be experiencing.

Things You'll Need:

- Quiet Space for Thinking
- A Writing Pad
- Any Writing Instrument

1.

Write down the probable cause of your creative block in the center of the page, i.e. "this scene isn't working." Or put it in the form of a question, i.e. "why isn't this scene working?" Draw a bubble or box around the question or statement. Note that this statement or question should probably be placed in the center of the page because it's the heart of your creative problem.

2.

Write down all related thoughts to the central problem, i.e. "the butler <u>character</u> is a cliché" or "the scene should be in an alley not a barn." These thoughts can be code, initials, sentences, phrases, doodles, or symbols. Draw bubbles or boxes around each related thought, and link these bubbles and boxes to the central bubble or box (and/or to each other, if appropriate).

3.

Above all, don't edit your thoughts. Write and draw everything that enters your mind. Each of the above series of bubbles or boxes may spawn yet more series of bubbles and boxes. When you run out of space on your page, you may want to start with a new page to draw a revised or brand new mind map.

4.

To break a creative block, you may need to draw a series of mind maps. The main goal is to move forward even if it's baby steps.

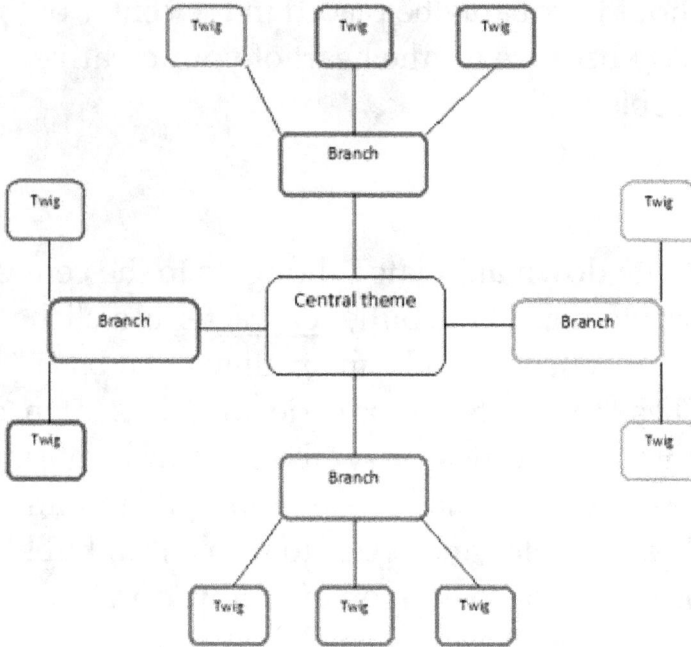

MIND MAP SAMPLE

Brainstorming Defined

Brainstorming is a process for developing creative solutions to problems, such as story difficulties, plotlines and character motivations. It is often used in companies and in team group sessions to come up with solutions for business problems.

Alex Faickney Osborn, an advertising manager, popularized the method in 1953 in his book, Applied Imagination. Ten years later, he proposed that teams could double their creative output with brainstorming (Osborn, 1963).

Brainstorming works by focusing on a problem, and then deliberately coming up with as many solutions as possible and by pushing the ideas as far as possible. One of the reasons it is so effective is that the brainstormers not only come up with new ideas in a session, but also spark off from associations with other people's ideas by developing and refining them.

While some research has found brainstorming to be ineffective, this seems more of a problem with the research itself than with the brainstorming tool (Isaksen, 1998).

There are four basic rules in brainstorming (Osborn, 1963) intended to reduce social inhibitions among team members, stimulate idea generation, and increase overall creativity:

◦No criticism: Criticism of ideas are withheld during the brainstorming session as the purpose is on generating varied and unusual ideals and extending or adding to these ideas. Criticism is reserved for the evaluation stage of the process. This allows the members to feel comfortable with the idea of generating unusual ideas.

◦Welcome unusual ideas: Unusual ideas are welcomed as it is normally easier to "tame down" than to "tame up" as new ways of thinking and looking at the world may provide better solutions.
◦Quantity Wanted: The greater the number of ideas generated, the greater the chance of producing a radical and effective solution.
◦Combine and improve ideas: Not only are a variety of ideals wanted, but also ways to combine ideas in order to make them better.

There are a number of easy brainstorming tactics writers can use to generate new ideas, including group brainstorming and using writing prompts. There are several tactics to using brainstorming in a way that benefits the writer and helps generate new ideas, thoughts and plot lines. Good brainstorming can help writers solve a number of serious problems, both with writer's block and in dealing with story issues.

Brainstorming Techniques

In school, many people are taught that brainstorming is simply making a list of ideas while writing them all down with as little stopping as possible. This rapid-fire type of brainstorming is sometimes effective, but there are other ways to brainstorm that can work in different ways.

The easiest way to brainstorm is indeed to create a list of ideas, statements or thoughts. However, the method and preparation can differ.

Keeping a notebook just for writing down ideas is a good way for many writers to keep track of their brainstorming sessions. This can also serve as a way to store ideas for use in other pieces of writing or newer stories.

Scott, a screenwriter in Hollywood, offers his technique for brainstorming:

Once I find a story concept I think might make a good movie, I create a Word file in my computer and start brainstorming ideas into that file. I can not emphasize enough how important brainstorming is. To begin with, this is where I discover if my concept is, indeed, good enough – if ideas for the plot and characters leap into my imagination, there's a pretty good chance I've got a strong concept.

Also, when I brainstorm, I start to 'see' the movie. Key scenes emerge, characters morph into being, I hear bits of dialogue. Of course, that all represents potential story stuff, but more than that, 'seeing' these elements fuels my passion... which drives me deeper into brainstorming... which gives me more story stuff... which gets me more excited. And so on.

Finally, and most importantly, if I do enough brainstorming and the creative stars align, this is where I uncover gold, those fantastic bits of story business that appear as if from nowhere, totally unexpected, surprising ideas and beats. The key to doing it right: no prejudgment. All ideas go into the master brainstorming file. Upon further reflection, I may choose to toss them aside - fine. But any image, scene, line of dialogue, action, or theme I have as I brainstorm goes into the file. I find this process frees up that special part of my consciousness so that those wondrous gold story nuggets can reveal themselves.

I spend days, even weeks brainstorming (in connection with research, our next subject). The process is a lot like wallowing in a sea of ideas, but again, this is where a majority of the story 'stuff' emerges and, more often than not, the Plotline and sub-plots start to show themselves, too.

Many aspiring screenwriters do not spend enough time brainstorming, their impatience getting the better of them. That will almost always come back to bite you in the ass. You'll either get stuck in the writing because you didn't 'find' your story or your story will have little, if anything special about it because you didn't brainstorm enough to surface the gold.

Free Association Techniques

Free association was primarily introduced for psychoanalytical purposes. Freud the originator of the free association technique used it mainly in his analysis of patients' conscious and sub-conscious thoughts. It is based on the free writing technique whereby individuals have the opportunity to write freely about their thoughts.

Free Association is used by specialist psychologist in the treatment or research of mental disorder. The patients are given the opportunity to express whatsoever comes into their mind. Feelings or thoughts should not be censored.

The aim of the analysis is mainly to help the individual to explore her/his inner thoughts. It is assumed in psychoanalysis that people are continuously in an antagonistic stage, whereby they are in conflict of the need to discover themselves (conscious, unconscious and preconscious) within their mind. Empirical research has shown that a trauma for an individual can act as resistance for him/her to express freely. Resistance was called by Freud as "Defenses".

Free Association is an unguided exercise, meaning that the thoughts derived are random and not necessarily directly interconnected. The outcomes of free association are unknown to parties, patient and therapist, when conducting the therapy. The intent of free association is not to bring back reminiscence. It is rather used to discover the self.

Sigmund Freud created this method mainly as an alternative to other practically weak methods being used. He did mainly use it in the study of self-analysis and interpretations of dreams. However, in the use of the self-discovering method, Freud concluded that certain sections of the mind remained completely repressed and unattainable to the conscious mind. Irrespective of the level of effort devoted. Freud's psychoanalysis was geared to dig up memories that were in conflict and thus as a consequent hidden deep within the mind. Free Association is widely used in the research of the brain (mind)

Free association can be used as a powerful tool to extract creativeness and innovation from the mind: It uses a combination of conglomerated idea-generation approaches. It can be classified into two sub sections being:

1.*Serial Association*

Serial Association can be considered as a step refinement search technique. There is an initial trigger (idea), once the thought is established in the mind each consecutive idea will be based on the initial trigger. This implies that ideas are derived from each other. One is built on one another, it continuous until a useful idea is developed.

2. *Centered Association*

Centered association or rather classical brainstorming is based on a trigger idea. The ideas that are a developed afterwards post to the introduction of the trigger idea are generated spontaneously and the ideas are not interrelated to one another (as shown in diagram below).This create a multiple of associated ideas.

The serial approach is used to explore and dig into a linear thought until you find something interesting. The centered approach is used to gather more ideas concerning a particular issue. It is geared at deriving alternative ideas in different direction compared to the serial approach; developing ideas in a linear vision.

All types of thoughts are to be revealed regardless of nature. Creativity is based on volatile and versatile ideas. The suppressed thoughts must thus be unveiled. Assuming that there isn't a specialized psycho-therapist at your-side, then either hire someone unknown or record it on tape (using record player). This makes the environment safe and sound for freedom of expression.

The rule is to intrigue your mind and associate your thought to an aim. The aim can be either serial or centered association.

It can be noticed that whether Free Association is used in psychoanalysis or in creative thinking it contributes to betterment of mental health. The technique is very alike F-R-E-E writing, the main difference is the absence of paper and psychological pressure. This method uses vocal expression of thoughts.

Rorschach Inkblot Test

The Rorschach test also known as the Rorschach inkblot test, the Rorschach technique, or simply the inkblot test) is a psychological test in which subjects' perceptions of inkblots are recorded and then analyzed using psychological interpretation, complex scientifically derived algorithms, or both. Some psychologists use this test to examine a person's personality characteristics and emotional functioning. It has been employed to detect an underlying thought disorder, especially in cases where patients are reluctant to describe their thinking processes openly. The test is named after its creator, Swiss psychologist Hermann Rorschach.

It can be used as a tool for accessing the creative unconscious by allowing the observer to assess the inkblots and come up with his own interpretation of what the ink blot represents. You can also observe the inkblots from the perspective of a plot or story idea, and some interesting and fun results can come from it.

There are a number of websites online that feature the Rorschach inkblots (and variations on them) and you can even make your own!

You can also view samples quickly by visiting Google Images and typing in ' Rorschach inkblot test.'

There is even a card game developed by Bucephalus games that uses a series of cards that looks pretty fun and interesting:

OH Cards

OH Cards are a genre of special playing cards used as story-telling prompters, counseling and psychotherapeutic tools, communication enhancers, educational aids, and social interactive games.

OH cards have no official or traditional interpretations of images, and instructions included with the decks encourage imaginative and personal interpretations of the images.

Usually these images are small paintings created by various artists specifically for this kind of use. As a genre, OH cards are unconventional "information containers", unbound books with no set sequence of pages.

Their most common uses are as a focus for self-examination and as prompters in social interactions. They are often used as aides in psychotherapeutic settings, and in a variety of educational situations. Less commonly, OH cards are used as catalysts in artistic fields: in writing, painting, theater, even dance.

Since their first publication in 1981 The OH Cards have become a widely acclaimed tool for personal and interpersonal work. Printed and sold in 20 different languages and in many more counties than that, they flow around the world much like a net of groundwater, supplying a resource to professionals of any teaching or healing denomination as well as countless interested private persons.

OH cards differ in artistic style and in content, so that children, youth, adults and seniors may find suitable images to trigger their own inner stories.

The OH Cards are designed to increase intuition, imagination, insight and inner vision. People around the world are using them to reclaim their sense of self and their place in this universe. One profound quality of this genre of "cards of association" is that they bend to the user: you can make them a tool for your own specific purpose. It is a mark of a great tool that it lends itself to universal application, and it is a mark of the power of these cards that they do this without imparting of dogma.

With OH you can anticipate to get in touch with your own stream of creativity and your processing skills. This increases awareness and the ability to positively influence private as well as professional situations.

Creativity by its very nature can't be induced or forced, but there are ways in which it can be trained. OH-cards can be applied to this objective.

Most people hear within themselves, with varying frequency or intensity, the voice of an inner critic. One function of this voice is to caution us about the leaving of familiar ways and conventions. But although such ways and conventions offer a safe place for the development of the personality they can also restrict spontaneity and the courage to live life in new ways.

The sheltered environment created by applying the OH-etiquette permits us to give free rein to our natural and innate creativity, to dream even an impossible dream. The images and words on the OH-cards provide the impulse that calls the idea forth, like a waking dream.

The OH-method of selecting cards randomly, rather than intentionally, prevents us from adhering only to the familiar. When the selected card is turned face up we are confronted with the unknown.

And as associations begin to flow in response to the image (or word, or combination of both), our innate faculty of imagination, wellspring of all new ideas, is activated. Experience has shown that even people who consider themselves uncreative can participate in this process and thereby learn to value their own inner wealth plus their ability to access it.

In addition to the random-access-effect, spontaneity plays a strong role in the OH-method. Trying to come up with an appropriate response through a rational process is not the avenue to self-accessing with OH. First respond, think about it or discuss it later!

OH-cards can also be used in an individual's search for creative solutions to specific problems. Through the process of associative play, in which one stands at a little distance to the actual problem, a whim or a flash of spontaneous inspiration might lead to an idea that wouldn't have occurred in the process of logical thinking usually applied to problem-solving. Such ideas can then be further examined for applicability.

Music

Many writers use music to free up their creative thoughts. Stephen King says he plays heavy rock and roll when he writes. I know of writers who can only write to instrumental classical music. Personally, I like soundtrack music of the New Age variety, dreamy spacey stuff, but only at certain times.

But music played over high quality earbuds can definitely stimulate the brain and get it firing on its creative side.

But beware distractions: it's not advised to play music over your computer, but use a separate -Ipod, MP3 player or CD player.

Sometimes you'll find your mind works best with no music at all: silence is golden for me much of the time, but when I get stuck I like to stimulate my brain with music.

Conclusion:

No matter how you approach your writing, it will improve as you learn to access your subconscious mind through the tools outlined in this book.

Show up each and every day at your writing space and be wholly in the moment of creation: make sure you are present when your muse arrives.

In your off hours, pursue books. Keep your brain stimulated with new ideas, fresh inspirations, as you stand on the shoulders of giants.

And remember the words of Stephen King:

"Great writers are great readers."

APPENDIX I

The following article is a wonderful example of the creative mind at work as it taps and explores subconscious themes.

The Creative Unconscious At Work:
The Films of Federico Fellini

"ITALIAN NEOREALISM"

Federico Fellini's major themes and expressions are not only symbolically shown through his characters human conditions, but are expressed through a psychoanalytic theory that was inspired by Carl Jung. Can the human condition be shown with realism in the Fellini's fantastical world of film? And if it does, what film has summed up his running theme of analyzing the psychosis of human conditions under NeoRealism and Fantasy?

8 1/2

8 ½ is a perfect summation of the filmmaking style of Federico Fellini. It highlights the Italian director's reason for juxtaposing the real with the imaginary, or the surreal. The scene, which

focuses on the psychological state of the character Guido, demonstrates Fellini's ability to use film as a tool for examining the human psyche.

He succeeds in creating scenery that is fantastic and ambiguous, but real and familiar, much like the mind. It should stand as no surprise that in his attempt to analyze the human condition, Fellini's work is informed by psychoanalytic theory, especially that of Carl Jung.

Through reflection and the use of dream imagery, Fellini investigates the stages of human development and the essential elements of personality. By examining the progression of work across his entire work of art, one can witness a separate form of development emerge.

Fellini's work matures as he weaves in and out of personal self-examination and relating characterization.

In order to understand the work of Federico Fellini, one must know a bit about Federico Fellini, the man. Many of the events and characters in his movies are drawn from his own life. Yet, Fellini has repeatedly insisted that none of his films are pure autobiography. Fellini was born on January 20, 1920 in the small town of Rimini, Italy. (www.tcm.com)

Roma (1972)

During his youth he worked as a cartoonist and later enrolled in college to avoid being drafted to the army. Fellini soon befriended Italian actor Aldo Fabrizi and the two formed a rather fruitful professional relationship. Together they wrote plays and acted. In the late 1930s,

Fellini wrote sketches for the radio program Cico e Pallina. Over the next decade, Fellini became more involved with film and began writing screenplays. In 1945 he worked alongside Roberto Rossellini on the film Roma, Citá Aperta. The movie was hailed an instant classic and is considered to be a defining moment in the history of Italian cinema. Roma, Citá Aperta was Fellini's first time to venture into the film movement known as Neo-Realism. (Kezich, 24-33)

Is Fellini's Fantastical World of Film Sure-Real?

NeoRealism began in the years following World War II as an alternative to the glamorous, fantastic stories being exported out of Hollywood.

The Neo-Realist filmmakers sought to inject realism into cinema by shooting in real-world, "on location" settings and by applying a documentary style approach to their work. The films to come out of this era deal with everyday social issues and often provide authentic depictions of life on the streets of Italy.

La Dolce Vita (1960)

His biggest success would come ten years later with the release of La Dolce Vita. The film, about the glamorous life in Rome, signaled a bit of a shift in the filmmaker's style. Though it was far from the fantasy of his later works, La Dolce Vita signaled a departure from the stark representation of Neo-Realism. (www.imdb.com)

After La Dolce Vita became a hit, Fellini was left with a bit of confusion over what his next project would be. Three years later, that exact uncertainty would be the basis of perhaps his finest film, 8 ½. The movie, which concerns the creative and personal struggle of a director named Guido, displayed a noticeably different composition than his previous work. It introduces elements of dreams, memories and fantastic images and sounds.

Satyricon (1969)

The study of psychoanalysis originated with the writings of Sigmund Freud. Among other things, Freud's sub-field of psychology examines the influence of childhood memories that are often repressed and a portion of the mind that we are not aware of called the sub-conscious.

He believed that through techniques such as free association, in which a person verbalizes everything that comes to mind, one could tap into the unconscious and confront memories and issues that lie within. Another major focus of psychoanalysis is the role of dreams. According to Freud, dreams are the pathway to the sub-conscious. Unsatisfied wishes, obsessions and anxieties all make their presence known through dreams. Though they are often encoded in symbols (or subtext), understanding dreams is a major step on the path towards awareness of the subconscious. (Freud, V. 19)

Another important influence on personality for Freud is sexuality. Freud wrote that all actions are dictated by drives, or impulses, whose roots are often grounded in sexuality. His concept of libido refers to the emotional and psychological energy that results from the biological drive of sexuality. I.E Satyricon

City Of Women (1980)

Freud identifies two categories of drives:

1. Eros refers to life impulses, those that "maintain life processes and ensure reproduction of the species. The key to these forces is the sexual drive, whose energy force is [the] libido." (Freud, V. 19)

2. Thanatos, on the other hand, reflects death impulses and is the source of aggressiveness. (Freud, V. 19)

Amarcord (1973)

The impact of psychoanalysis on the world of art has been very important. The movement known as surrealism, which began in the 1920s, is directly influenced by psychoanalytic theory regarding dreams. Ironically, the form of art that guarantees the truest depiction of reality became the ideal venue for exploring dreams and the fantastic. Fellini was aware of all of this when he decided on his filmmaking style with and+Amarcord', wrapperClassName: 'title bar', src: 'http://filmdirectors.co/wp-content/plugins/imdb-link-transformer/inc/popup.php?film=8+½+and+Amarcord' });" href="#" title="open a new window with IMDb informations">8 ½ and Amarcord. However, it wasn't the writings of Freud that he looked to for inspiration, but those of one of his contemporaries, Carl Jung.

Fellini was first introduced to the theories of Jung by an analyst friend, Ernst Bernhard. He was immediately drawn to Jung's work regarding dreams and his treatment of symbols. Bernhard guided Fellini through his studies and encouraged him to keep a dream journal of his own. For

Fellini, this journal served as a way to openly explore his creativity and to work out ideas that would occasionally appear in his films.

Jung's work is often met with controversy as it draws upon fields not normally associated with psychology, including religion. Jung concerned himself with the unconscious and its effect on human drives and emotions, but he also introduced a new concept, the collective unconscious.

According to Jung, there exists a portion of the unconscious that is shared by all people. Though individual's language and ways of expressing emotions may differ, the emotions themselves remain the same. If this isn't enough to give examples on Fellini's editing and shooting styles, within the collective unconscious lie images known as archetypes. (Jung, 12-65)

Federico Fellini
These archetypes are universal thoughts or predispositions to respond to the world in certain ways. Though they never fully enter consciousness, the archetypes appear in symbolic form through art (or what I know as SUBTEXT), myths and dreams. Jung believed that it is important to understand these archetypes because they represent the latent potential of the psyche

and our individual potential to become part of a larger, universal experience. (Jung, 12-65)

Fellini's interest in Jung was crucial to the development of his filmmaking style. In 8 ½ "dreams and fantasies represented a way of gaining access to an imaginative world of greater significance", otherwise known as the collective unconscious.

The symbols contained in the collective unconscious provided Fellini with a new vocabulary of imagery that could be used to appeal to viewers on an emotional, rather than simply visual level. This, I believe is why, the use of montages are overtly used throughout 8 ½.

When asked about the inspiration in his themes, Fellini provided the following response:

"What do we mean by inspiration? The capacity for making direct contact between your unconscious and your rational mind. When an artist is happy and spontaneous, he is successful because he reaches the unconscious and translates it with a minimum of interference…

The transformation from dream to film takes place in the awakened conscious state, and it's clear that consciousness involves intellectual presumption which detracts from creativity." (Murray)

8 ½ opens with the scene, in which the character Guido struggles to get out of his smoke-filled car and finds himself soaring through the air. The scene emphasizes Guido's anxieties, both creative and personal. Guido feels the pressure of creating his movie of utopia and finds himself at somewhat of a creative drought.

When he is pulled back down to Earth by the press agent on the beach, the mechanisms of film are bringing him back to reality. This would be the definitive moment in the film where montage is used to sum up the human condition from a parallel psychoanalytical form of fantasy and realism.

It is difficult to imagine what a Fellini work might appear as, if it weren't for his experiences with psychoanalysis. His interest in dreams and the writings of Carl Jung dictated his choice to begin filming fantasy, starting with 8 ½. Fellini films work mainly because they relate so well to the human condition.

Ironically, through the depiction of dreams and fantasy, Fellini achieved a level of realism that could never be attained with neo-realism alone. By using himself as a subject, his films strike a comprehensive range of knowledge in tapping into the collective unconscious of the viewer.

APPENDIX II

Essays On The Creative Unconscious

The study of creativity and the unconscious is a complex mix of scientific disciplines that walk the worlds of Psychology, Physiology and even the metaphysical and paranormal realms of Mythology, Occultism and beyond.

Some like to approach the subject in a scholarly manner, others prefer to simply tap into the power of it and not question the theories or science behind it.

In the following section I offer some sources to the former:

An Overview of Art and the Creative Unconscious by Erich Neumann - An Essay and Review by Gregory Hayes

Art and the Creative Unconscious by Erich Neumann, originally published as Kunst und schöpferisches Unbewusstes some fifty-four years ago, is a thorough, if at times somewhat abstract and male-centric journey into the realms of creativity and the unconscious.

Throughout this collection of four essays, Neumann displays the articulate and thoughtful demeanor that has made him one of Carl Jung's most distinguished students. Throughout, Neumann dissects the intersections of creativity, culture, and the unconscious, in a deft attempt at illuminating the inner motivation of some of Europe's most famous creative men. Framing his view of creativity and the unconscious using examples strongly rooted within Western cultural tradition and mythology, Neumann introduces the reader to the individual and collective unconscious and archetypes of the creative man.

He illustrates his understanding of the tension and transformative power of creativity through some of Europe's most renowned male geniuses: Leonardo da Vinci, Marc Chagall, Rainer Maria Rilke, and Johann Wolfgang von Goethe. In the first essay, Leonardo da Vinci and the Mother Archetype, Neumann explores at length the life and creativity of Leonardo da Vinci. Neumann suggests: "Leonardo fascinates us very much in the same way as Goethe, precisely because we here encounter a striving for a life of individuation, a life of wholeness" (p. 4).

Throughout this essay, Neumann uses what he conceives of as a transpersonal approach which explores the relations between Leonardo's creativity, life development, and what the author sees as a struggle to create meaning in a world where the artist does not always fit in.

Neumann frames a theory of Leonardo's massive and transformational creativity by including, at length, a discussion of one of the artist's earliest memories of a dream like vision, as well as a discussion of several of his masterpieces.

Like Jung, by focusing on Leonardo's vision and the archetypal qualities of his paintings, by weaving together Egyptian mythology and the content of Leonardo's creativity, Neumann develops a frame in which to explore creativity in relation to the unconscious and the transpersonal.

Neumann builds upon a theory of understanding creativity through a lens that delineates between feminine and masculine, that which Neuman calls the "Great Mother" and the "Great Father" archetypes (p, 23). He posits throughout that the great creative men of Western culture typically are drawn forth toward exceptional creative expression via the strong unconscious pull of the feminine archetype. Whereas, Neumann argues that the men who settle into dominantly expected cultural life patterns have often repressed the feminine side of their internal selves, men of great creative expression are drawn toward the branches of creative possibility in order to give voice to the feminine aspects of their unconscious selves.

This, Neumann includes, often creates great turmoil within the life of a creative man; surely even more so in the often rigid gender paradigms of Neumann's era. However, even today, especially in those areas where cultural gestalts severely limit the acceptable expression of men and women into particular roles – and, perhaps to a lesser degree, in all of Western culture – Neumann's concept of the expression of creative genius erupting from the unconscious struggle to give voice to the archetypes is worthy of close inspection by any student of creativity, culture, and transformation.

In the second essay, Art and Time Neumann explores the relation between culture, era, and creativity, and suggests that "Our present inquiry lies within the psychology of cultures; it aims at an understanding of art as a psychological phenomenon of central importance to the collectivity as well as the individual" (p. 81).

Neumann frames his ideas by including the collective unconscious as the origin of all psychic activity, a formless background from which all consciousness and culture spring:

"For primitive and early cultures, the creative force of the numinosum supports or even engenders consciousness: it brings differentiation and order into an indeterminate world driven by chaotic powers and enables man to orient himself" (p. 85).

Neumann sees the substratum of unconsciousness as a creative force welling up in the individual and collective consciousness of humankind.

Within the structure of Art and Time, Neumann develops his concepts of an "integral psychic field" (p. 88) within which members of a culture find and demonstrate meaning whereby, via the juxtaposition and interaction of the collective unconscious and the collective conscious, negotiate their way through the accepted canons, rites, believes, lifeways, and values of the group. Leaders considered faithful to the approved canons or beliefs of the time fit and demonstrate alignment with the expectations of the collective.

Those individuals who question the collective are viewed during their time as rule breakers, outsiders, or worse. Often, the latter group includes those affecting the deepest transformations of culture and society; those demonstrating the most creative genius. Neumann articulates this idea via the notion of the "epiphany of the numinosum" (p. 87): the genuine and totally original creativity that explodes or erupts as an unexpected, unforeseen revelation.

In this light, the most profound creativity may be seen by the dominant culture as valuable or dangerous depending upon perspective.

Neumann concludes that the creativity that is accepted by the culture "resembles the digging and walling in of deep wells, around which the group gathers and from whose water it lives" (p. 92). When the great creative epiphanies are not accepted by the group, one may be shunned or violently driven away.

Thus the tension formed between culture and creative expression, illuminated by Neumann's articulate exploration, can inform our present movement into an age of chaos and creativity by giving us footholds upon which to stand above and beyond the singular perspective of one culture or one individual.

For, as Neumann so eloquently states about profoundly creative individuals: "Their secret alchemy achieves a synthesis of the numinosum at the heart of nature and psyche" (p. 103). This creative synthesis surely is a key toward a graceful and ecologically sustainable transformation of our times.

As we have said, with profound creativity comes great tension. Creativity is rooted most solidly in the tension of the inner and the outer worlds of the

individual, the culture, and humanity in the largest sense possible. These tensions often create chaos, dissolution, and disintegration. The same tension that is the root of creativity, Neumann argues, leads often in our world to neurosis and sickness, individually and culturally: "We know that the core of the neurosis of our time is the religious problem or, stated in more universal terms, the search for the self. In this sense neuroses, like the mass phenomena resulting from this situation, are a kind of sacred disease. Our whole epoch is full of it, but behind it stands the power of a numinous center,
which seems to direct not only the normal development of the individual, but his psychic crises and transformations as well – not only the disease but also the cure, both in the individual and in the collective" (pp. 132-3).

In the third essay, Note on Marc Chagall, Neumann illuminates his belief that in a cruel and destructive world, in which the truly aware human understands and feels deeply the horrors and sufferings of his or her time, the creative individual will find solace and expression in the heart of our common unitary reality.

He suggests that individuals with Chagall's brilliance evidence transcendent expression where "geysers of creativity spurt from the tortured soil" (p. 147). He suggests that the divine and human are travelling upon the same road, enveloped within the same unitary reality.

One finishes the essay with the understanding that Neumann saw no schism between this reality and another. Rather, in the truly creative person, including Neumann himself, an understanding of the non-dual nature of reality, discussed by so many mystics and masters, is illumined within the creativity which flows forth from the psychologically balanced individual.

Neumann's last essay, Creative Man and Transformation, is a very profound examination of the roots of creativity within cultures and individuals, and the relation between an effective integration of the unconscious and the conscious within the individual, and the collective unconscious and collective conscious aspects of the cultural canon or group.

It is interesting and very appropriate here that Neumann compares the forces of the psyche that lead to neurosis. Within this essay, Neumann gives example to the closing down of flexibility within our realities which in extreme cases lead to a kind of "sclerosis of consciousness" (p. 160). Here an individual is so consumed by the ideals of culture or ego that one loses the ability to approach the totality of self in all of its manifestations.

The culture may, through expectations and rules begin to develop in the individual an ideal egoistic self that is not congruent to the whole self at all. This then leads, in Neumann's view, to a sublimation of the potentialities of the whole self, toward the more rigid expectations or lifeways common in the local cultural environment:

"In the sclerotic consciousness typical of our cultural situation, we have a radicalization of the ego and ego ideal; egoistic separation from the living unconscious and loss of the self have become an acute danger" (p, 161). According to Neumann, within this hemmed in, rigidified consciousness, one finds dangerously locked-in emotions and psychic energies.

He utilizes the metaphor of a fiery and molten underworld contained by an inflexible shell to express the result of this rigidity where the often chaotic movements of the unseen unconscious are locked within, closed off from awareness.

Within this way of thinking, though rigidity may seem to provide a safe haven from the chaotic nature of the unconscious underworld, we at times may witness the rumblings, fracture, or bubbling up of repressed psychic energy.

Creative transformation of the individual, Neumann includes, must rather be rooted in a dynamic synthesis within the totality of the individual where conscious and unconscious aspects of self can inter-relate fluidly and dynamically.

Here "the clearest, though not the only, indication of psychic transformation is a change in the relation to extrapsychic reality" (p. 166). One senses the perspective of thou toward self and world and the polarization of opposites transforms toward unity.

Thus, although Neumann wrote for an earlier generation, we may find inspiration in his at times eloquent illumination of creativity and transformation being the essence of the fully mature individual and culture. In our continuing time of chaos and violence, we may find solace in the concept of creative transformation as a full expression of personal and cultural well-being. Our present zeitgeist appears to mirror that which Neumann explored more than fifty years ago. For the student of creativity and transformation, Erich Neumann's Art and the Creative Unconscious comes highly recommended.

Recommended Reading:

Zen In The Art Of Writing - Ray Bradbury

Writing Down the Bones - Natalie Goldberg

The Courage to Create - Rollo May

Art and the Creative Unconscious - Erich Neumann

Memories, Dreams, Reflections - C.G. Jung

Drawing the Light from Within:

Keys to Awaken Your Creative Power - Judith Cornell

The Creative Spirit - Daniel Goleman, Paul Kaufman

Dream Work: Techniques for Discovering the Creative Power In Dreams - Jeremy Taylor

The Widening Stream: The Seven Stages Of Creativity - David Ulrich

Creativity Revealed: Discovering the Source - Scott Jeffrey/David R. Hawkins

Becoming A Writer - Dorothea Brande

The Power of Your Subconscious Mind - Joseph Murphy

On Writing - Stephen King

Techniques of the Selling Writer - Dwight V. Swain

www.ingramcontent.com/pod-product-compliance
Lightning Source LLC
Chambersburg PA
CBHW072139270326
41931CB00010B/1816